TV & VIDEO

Christopher Griffin-Beale and Robyn Gee

Contents

2 The TV revolution

4 Broadcasting

6 TV and video cameras

8 Colour cameras

9 Television sound

10 In a TV studio

12 In the control room

14 Transmitting TV pictures

16 TV sets

18 Outside the studios

20 Recording and editing

22 Special electronic effects

24 Digital effects

26 TV and computers

28 Home video equipment

30 Using a video camera

31 TV in the future

32 Index

Illustrated by
Ian Stephen, Graham Round,

Graham Smith, Philip Schramm, Joe McEwan, Clifford Meadway

and Martin Salisbury

Designed by Graham Round, Kim Blundell and Roger Priddy

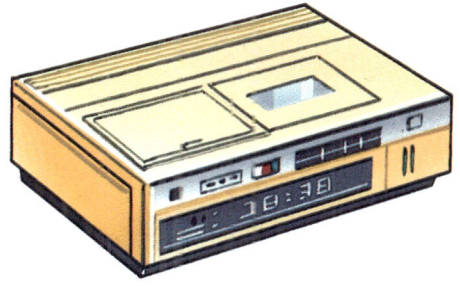

The TV revolution

Fifty years ago it seemed miraculous that pictures and sound could be sent through the air. The TV system used today was developed during the 1930s, and the 1950s saw the first TV revolution, with TV reaching millions of homes and the establishment of more companies to broadcast to them. In the last few years another TV revolution has begun. This new revolution is about the use to which a TV can be put and the choices that are available to the viewer. It has been brought about by great advances in technology, above all by the invention of micro chips. "Chips" have made video equipment and computers small, cheap and reliable enough to be used at home and this has greatly extended the scope of television. As you can see from this page, the pictures on your screen can now come from a great variety of sources other than broadcasting companies. You can find out more about all the things mentioned on this page elsewhere in the book.

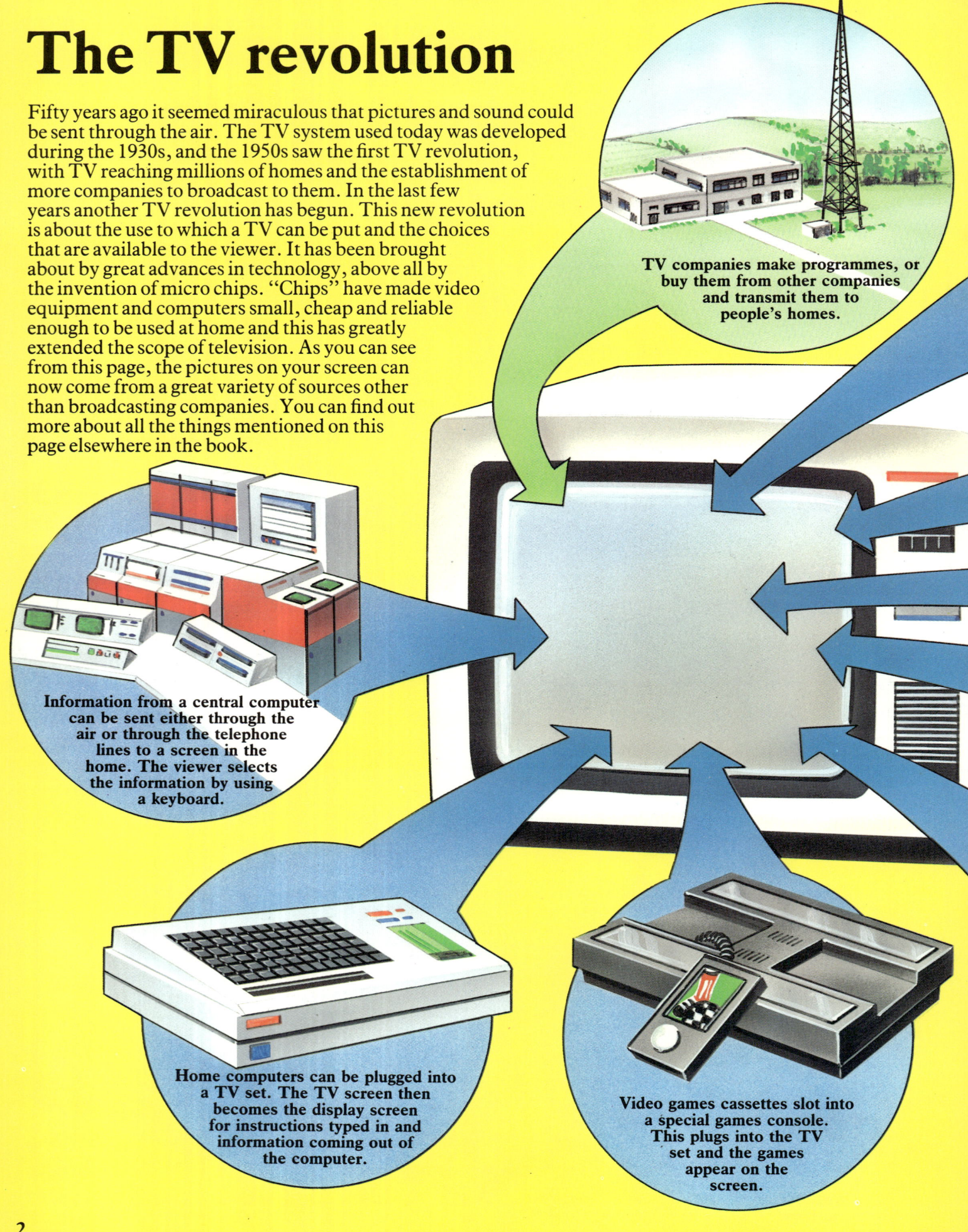

TV companies make programmes, or buy them from other companies and transmit them to people's homes.

Information from a central computer can be sent either through the air or through the telephone lines to a screen in the home. The viewer selects the information by using a keyboard.

Home computers can be plugged into a TV set. The TV screen then becomes the display screen for instructions typed in and information coming out of the computer.

Video games cassettes slot into a special games console. This plugs into the TV set and the games appear on the screen.

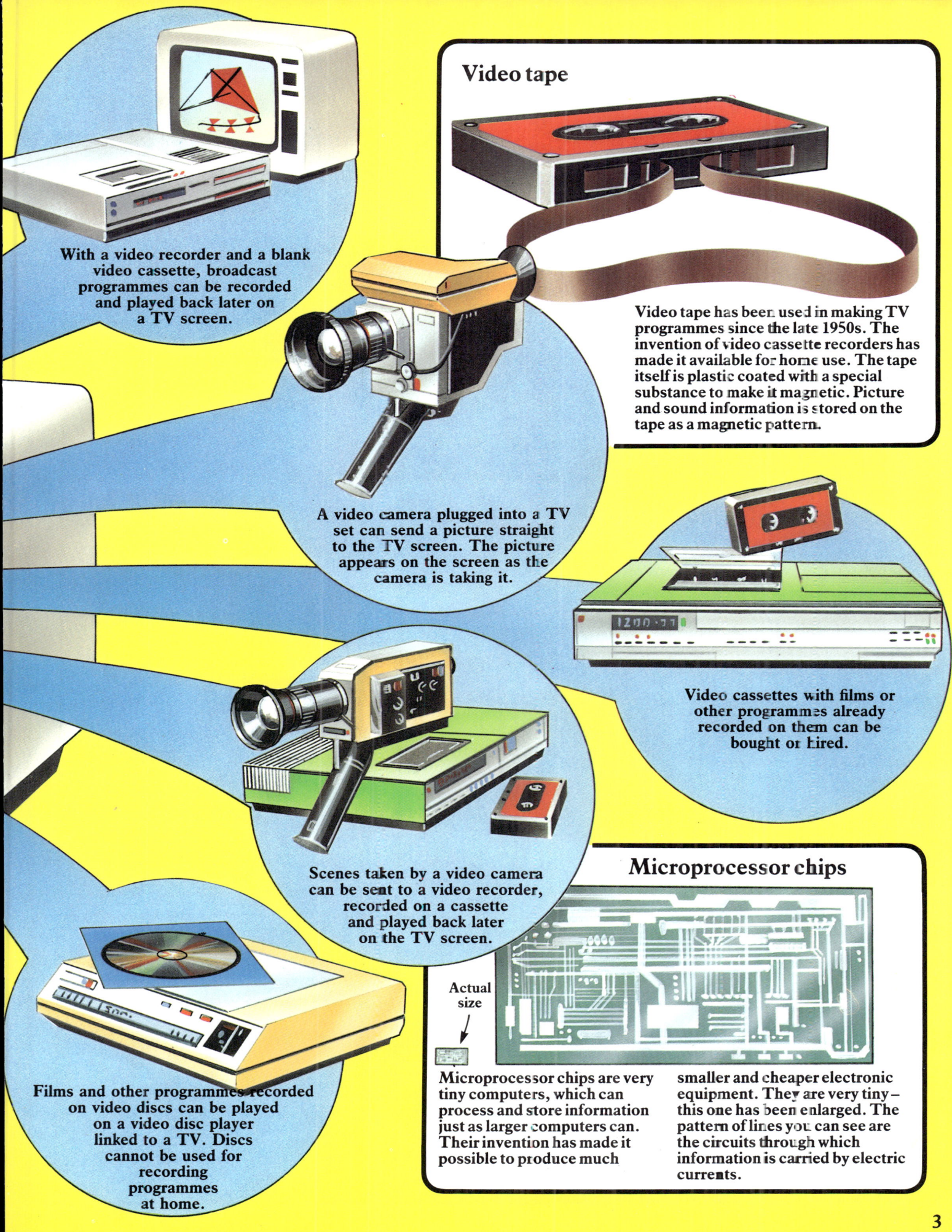

With a video recorder and a blank video cassette, broadcast programmes can be recorded and played back later on a TV screen.

Video tape

Video tape has been used in making TV programmes since the late 1950s. The invention of video cassette recorders has made it available for home use. The tape itself is plastic coated with a special substance to make it magnetic. Picture and sound information is stored on the tape as a magnetic pattern.

A video camera plugged into a TV set can send a picture straight to the TV screen. The picture appears on the screen as the camera is taking it.

Video cassettes with films or other programmes already recorded on them can be bought or hired.

Scenes taken by a video camera can be sent to a video recorder, recorded on a cassette and played back later on the TV screen.

Microprocessor chips

Actual size

Microprocessor chips are very tiny computers, which can process and store information just as larger computers can. Their invention has made it possible to produce much smaller and cheaper electronic equipment. They are very tiny – this one has been enlarged. The pattern of lines you can see are the circuits through which information is carried by electric currents.

Films and other programmes recorded on video discs can be played on a video disc player linked to a TV. Discs cannot be used for recording programmes at home.

3

Broadcasting

TV broadcasting is the process of sending out pictures and sound through the air. It developed out of two other important inventions: cinema photography (a way of capturing and reproducing moving images) and radio broadcasting (a way of sending sound through the air on radio waves). Once people had discovered how to adapt these two systems to make radio waves carry moving pictures as well as sound, "tele-vision" (literally "seeing at a distance") had been invented.

All the broadcast pictures you see on your TV screen are either "live", which means that the action is happening at the same time as you are seeing it, or "prerecorded", that is recorded before being broadcast. Prerecorded pictures are recorded either on film by a cine camera, or on videotape by a TV camera. Some programmes are made up of a mixture of live and prerecorded pictures.

Live programmes

In the early days of television all programmes were broadcast live. Now most are recorded before being broadcast. Those that still go out live are the ones where it is important to use the very latest information. Even live programmes are usually recorded during broadcasting, so that there is a copy to refer to or to show again.

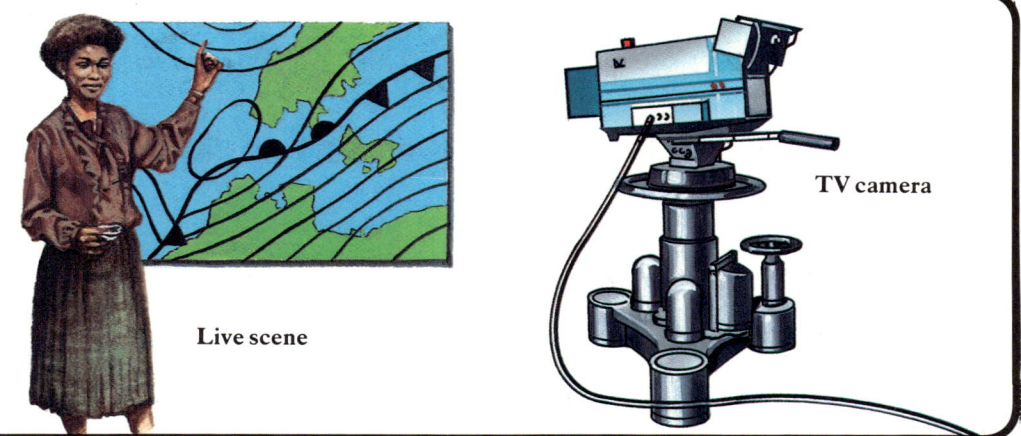

Live scene

TV camera

Prerecording on video tape

Video tape recording has been used in television for more than twenty years. Microphones and TV cameras send information to video tape recorders where it is stored on magnetic tape very similar to that used in sound recorders. Prerecorded tapes are stored in a video tape room ready to be played back when it is time to broadcast them. Mistakes can be cut out and new bits put in before it is broadcast.

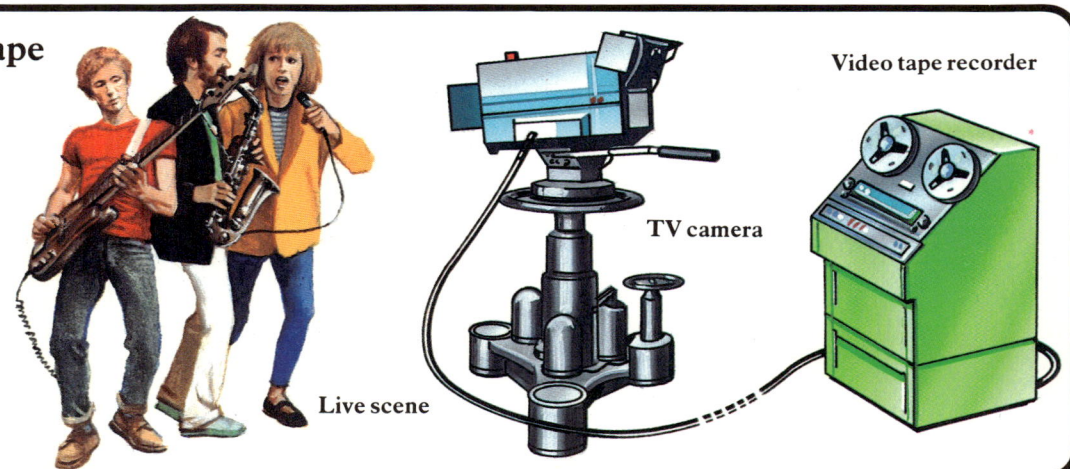

Video tape recorder

TV camera

Live scene

Prerecording on film

Some programmes are recorded on film. In this case the picture is recorded on plastic coated with a light sensitive chemical which has to be developed before it can be used. To broadcast material recorded on film, it has to be run through a telecine machine. This converts the film images into electronic signals which can then be broadcast in the same way as the electronic signals straight from TV cameras.

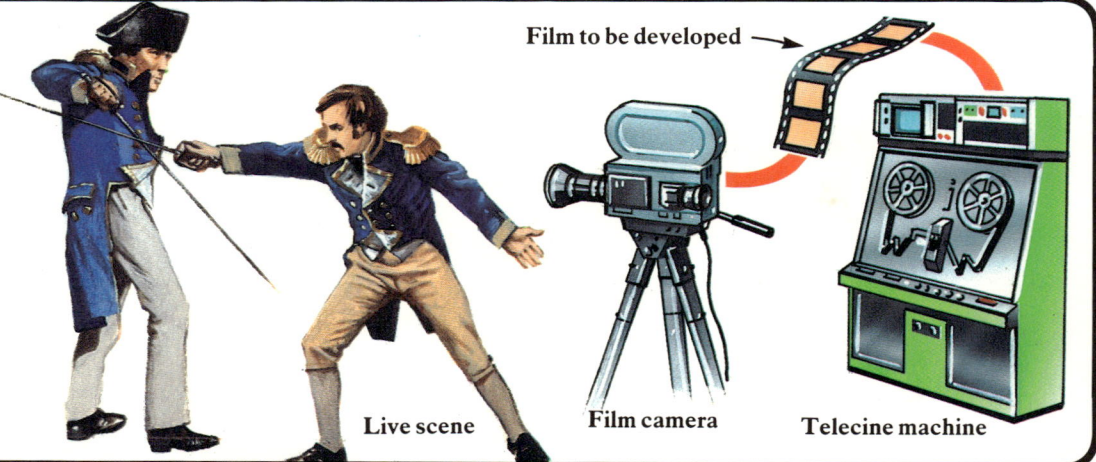

Film to be developed →

Live scene

Film camera

Telecine machine

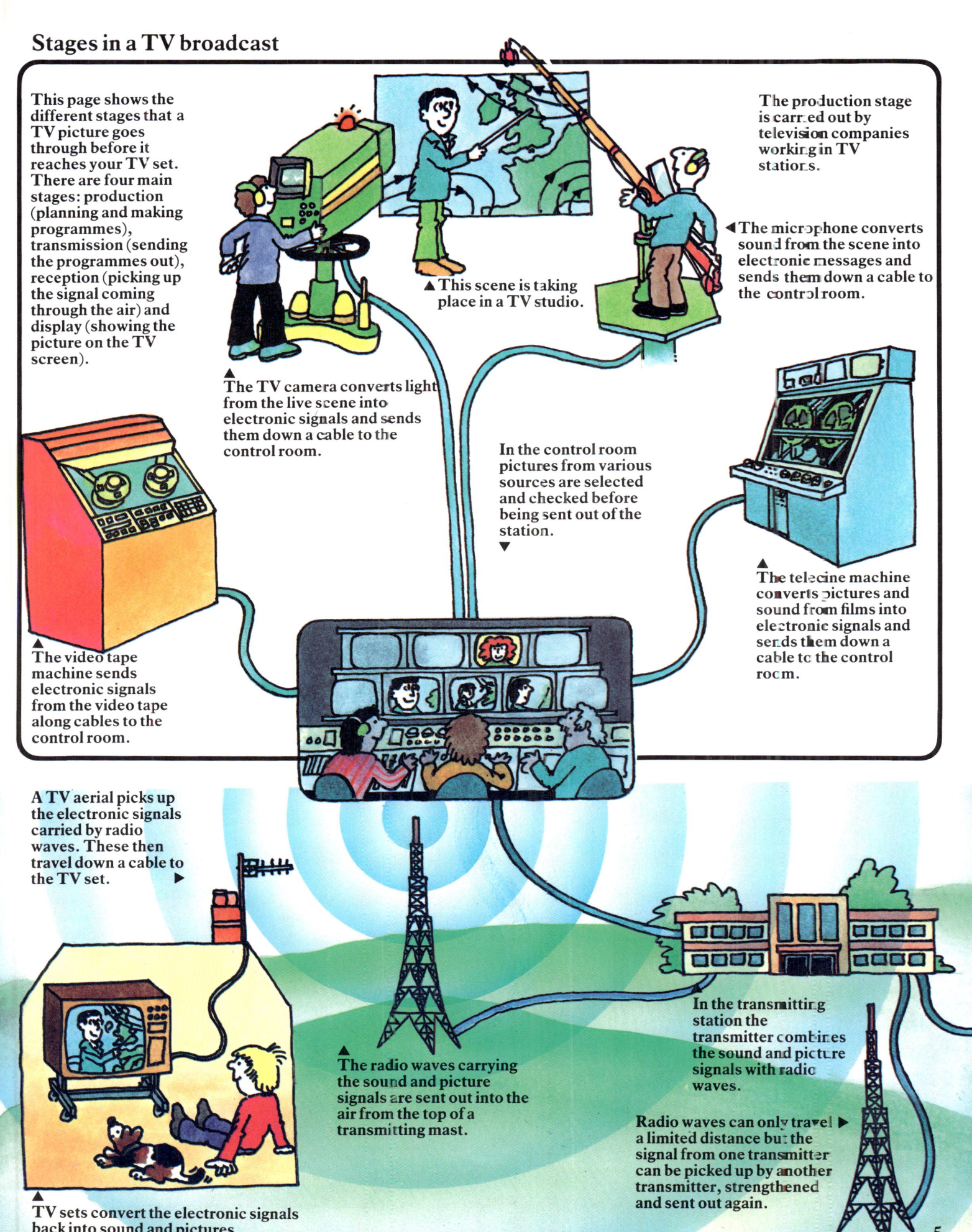

Stages in a TV broadcast

This page shows the different stages that a TV picture goes through before it reaches your TV set. There are four main stages: production (planning and making programmes), transmission (sending the programmes out), reception (picking up the signal coming through the air) and display (showing the picture on the TV screen).

▲ This scene is taking place in a TV studio.

The production stage is carried out by television companies working in TV stations.

◄ The microphone converts sound from the scene into electronic messages and sends them down a cable to the control room.

The TV camera converts light from the live scene into electronic signals and sends them down a cable to the control room.

In the control room pictures from various sources are selected and checked before being sent out of the station.
▼

▲ The telecine machine converts pictures and sound from films into electronic signals and sends them down a cable to the control room.

▲ The video tape machine sends electronic signals from the video tape along cables to the control room.

A TV aerial picks up the electronic signals carried by radio waves. These then travel down a cable to the TV set. ►

In the transmitting station the transmitter combines the sound and picture signals with radio waves.

The radio waves carrying the sound and picture signals are sent out into the air from the top of a transmitting mast.

Radio waves can only travel ► a limited distance but the signal from one transmitter can be picked up by another transmitter, strengthened and sent out again.

▲ TV sets convert the electronic signals back into sound and pictures.

5

TV and video cameras

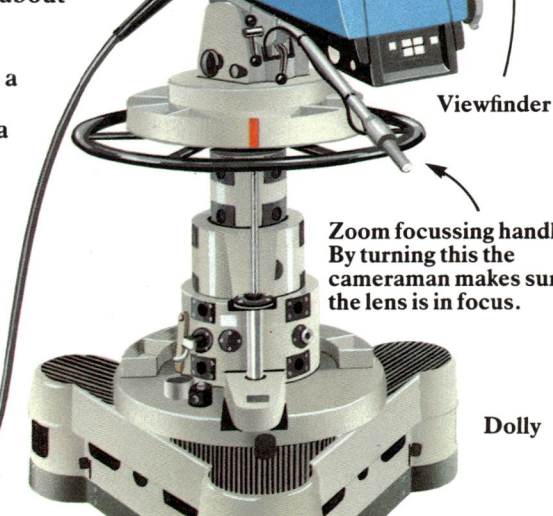

Lens

Viewfinder

Zoom focussing handle. By turning this the cameraman makes sure the lens is in focus.

Dolly

Cable taking electric signals to control room

TV cameras are electronic. They work by turning light into electric currents, which are sent out of the cameras along electric cables. There is no film or tape inside them.

The electric currents can either be sent to a transmitter to be broadcast through the air on radio waves, or they can be sent to a video tape recorder to be stored and transmitted later. They are often transmitted and recorded at the same time.

A video camera works like a TV camera, but is smaller and lighter.

TV cameras come in various different types and sizes. They look quite like film cameras, but they are usually much bigger. The ones used in TV studios are often mounted on wheeled stands called dollies, so that they can be moved about easily.

Most TV cameras nowadays have a zoom lens. This allows the cameraman to alter his view from a long-shot to a close-up very fast. For the viewer this gives the impression that you are zooming towards the subject.

The picture taken by a TV camera can appear on a TV screen at almost the exact instant that it is being taken. The viewfiender of the camera is, in fact, a miniature TV screen. The picture that the cameraman sees there has already been taken and processed by the camera.

Viewfinder

Cheaper cameras have an "optical" viewfinder, like those in still cameras. More expensive cameras have "electronic" viewfinders (mini TV screens) as in TV cameras.

Most video cameras have a zoom lens, which is either power-operated or hand-operated. Some also have a macro lens. This allows you to shoot subjects very close to the lens without going out of focus.

Handle for holding camera

Video cameras can be divided into three main groups. There are those designed for home use, like the one above, with which you can make your own programmes, record them on video cassettes and show them on your TV. There are video cameras designed for use in industry and education, which are slightly more complicated and produce better pictures. There are also video cameras designed to produce pictures to be broadcast, which are very similar to traditional TV cameras but much lighter and more manoeuvrable.

Camera tubes

The part of a camera that changes light into an electric current is called the tube. In a black and white camera there is one tube; in colour cameras there are usually three.

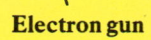

Electron gun

Target plate

At one end there is a metal plate called the target plate. At the other end is a device called an electron gun. You can see how the tube works on the opposite page.

Turning light into electric messages

To turn a scene into a picture on a TV screen, a TV camera has to convert the entire scene into a series of electric messages. It does this by turning light from the scene into electricity. TV sets turn the electricity back into pictures. It is easiest to understand how a camera works by first looking at how it converts scenes into black and white pictures.

1

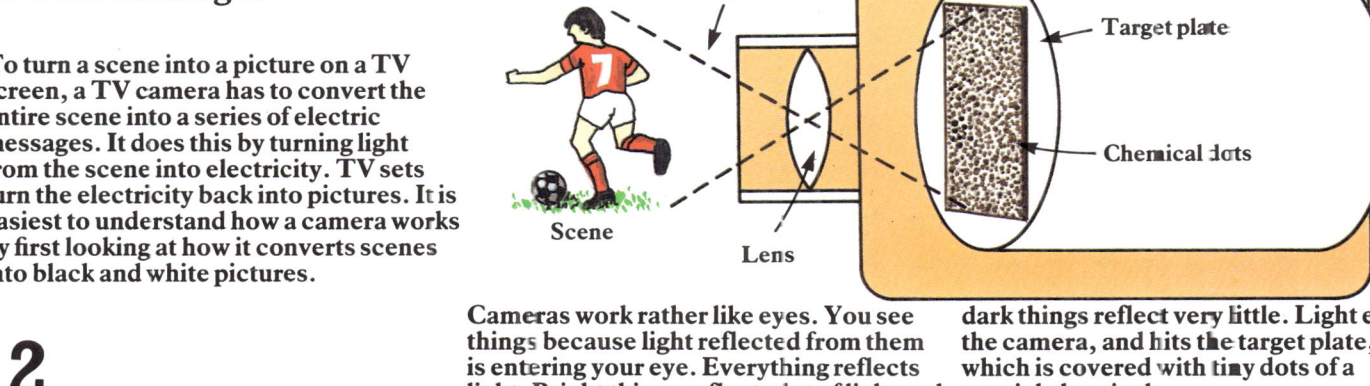

Cameras work rather like eyes. You see things because light reflected from them is entering your eye. Everything reflects light. Bright things reflect a lot of light and dark things reflect very little. Light enters the camera, and hits the target plate, which is covered with tiny dots of a special chemical.

2

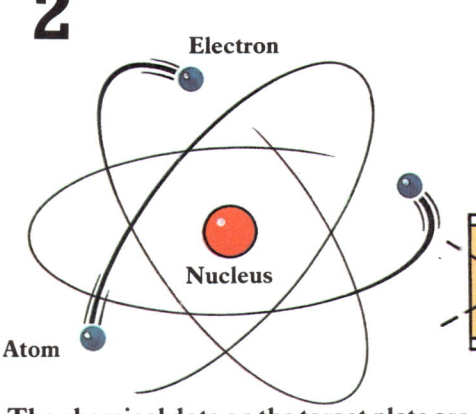

The chemical dots on the target plate are sensitive to light. When light hits them they react by releasing electrons (part of the atoms of which everything in the world is made). All atoms have a nucleus in the middle with electrons spinning round it. Each nucleus and each electron carries a tiny bit of electricity called a charge. A nucleus has a positive charge and an electron has a negative charge. Sometimes electrons split away from the nucleus leaving the atom with a positive charge.

3

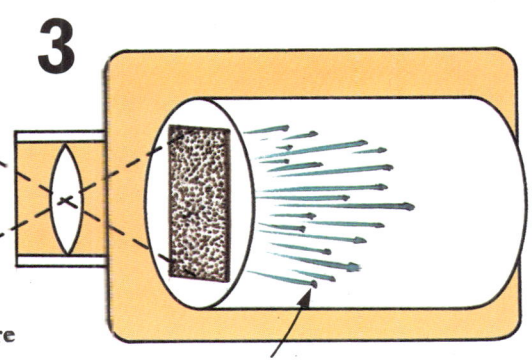

Electrons escaping from target plate

When light falls on the chemical dots the electrons they release flow in the direction of the target plate. The size of the flow depends on the brightness of the light falling on each dot. The flow affects the atoms in the target plate and makes electrons escape down the tube.

4

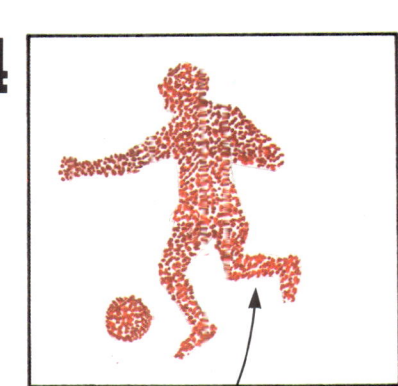

Pattern of positive charges

Since electrons carry a negative charge, this leaves a pattern of positive charges on the back of the target plate. This now contains all the information necessary to reproduce the scene on a TV screen, but the information still needs to be carried out of the camera.

Taking the messages out of the camera

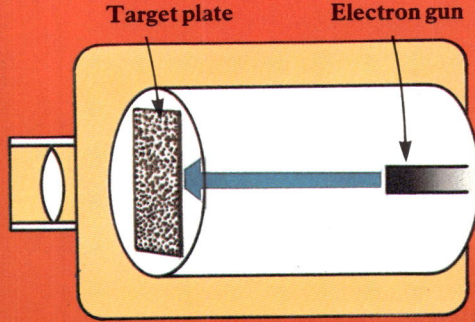

Target plate   Electron gun

The electron gun is the device which interprets the information on the target plate and sends it out of the camera. It "reads" or scans the target plate by shooting a rapid stream of electrons down the tube towards it.

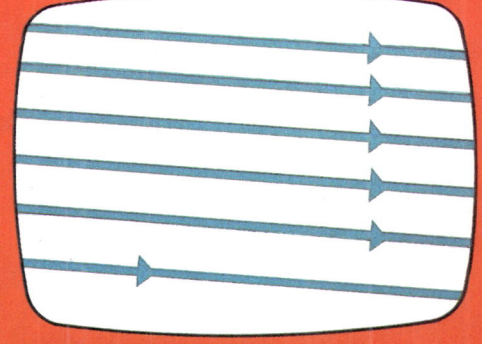

Lines show path of electron gun.

This diagram shows the path in which the stream of electrons moves over the target plate. It moves from left to right and from top to bottom in rather the same way as your eyes read the words on a page. It actually takes 625 lines (525 in the system used in America and Japan) to read the target plate from top to bottom and this only takes 1/25th of a second each time.

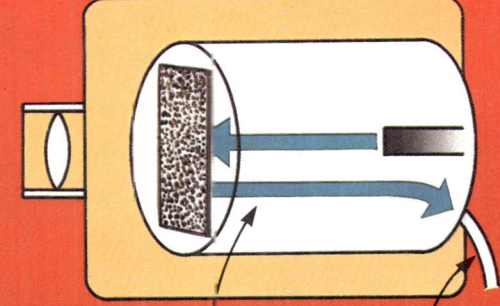

Stream of electrons returning   Cable

After hitting the target plate the stream of electrons returns down the tube. But where light from the original scene has made electrons escape from the plate, electrons from the stream replace them. This makes the returning stream vary in strength according to the brightness of the original scene. The stream of electrons passes out of the camera down a cable.

Colour cameras

Colour TV and video cameras work like black and white cameras, but they translate colours, as well as brightness, into electrical messages. To do this they have three camera tubes instead of one. Light entering the camera is split up into three key colours – red, green and blue – known as the primary colours of light. By mixing them together in various combinations and proportions you can produce any other colour, or even white. The three separate streams of light are directed on to the three separate camera tubes, which turn them into electric signals.

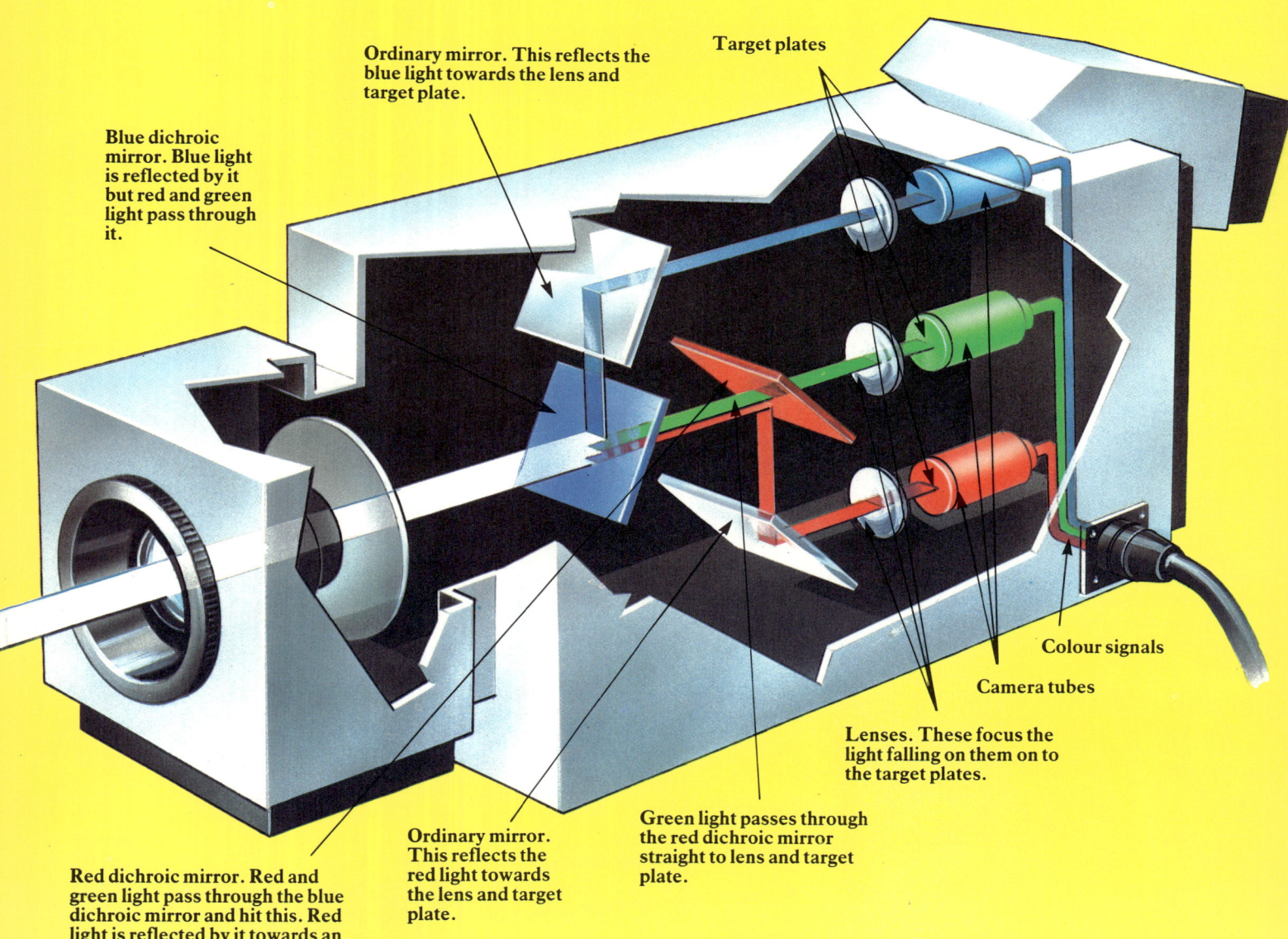

Ordinary mirror. This reflects the blue light towards the lens and target plate.

Target plates

Blue dichroic mirror. Blue light is reflected by it but red and green light pass through it.

Colour signals

Camera tubes

Lenses. These focus the light falling on them on to the target plates.

Green light passes through the red dichroic mirror straight to lens and target plate.

Ordinary mirror. This reflects the red light towards the lens and target plate.

Red dichroic mirror. Red and green light pass through the blue dichroic mirror and hit this. Red light is reflected by it towards an ordinary mirror.

Special "dichroic" mirrors split up all the light entering the camera into three separate streams of red, green and blue light. The three streams are each directed through three separate lenses on to three target plates. The target plates are then scanned by electron guns in exactly the same way as the target plate in a black and white camera is scanned. This produces three streams of electrical information, representing the brightness of each of the colours at each point in the picture. The three streams are then combined together to form one signal.

This is called the "luminance" signal. It conveys only variations of light and shade and can be received by black and white, as well as colour TV sets. Colour information (two "chrominance" signals combined together) is superimposed on top of this basic signal. Colour sets can decode this information and use it to add colour to the luminance signal.

There are different systems for coding the colour information on to the basic black and white signal. Most parts of Western Europe use a system called PAL; the French system is called SECAM; and the American system is NTSC. Other parts of the world have adopted one of these three systems.

Some video cameras have only one tube. The target plate is coated with a pattern of three kinds of dot. Each of which responds only to one of the three primary colours.

Television sound

A microphone turns sound into electronic signals, rather as a camera turns light into electronic signals. The sound signals can be stored on tape with the picture signals or transmitted immediately through the air on radio waves.

Various different types of microphone are used in making TV programmes. The type used depends on the situation and the kind of sound to be picked up. Sometimes as many as 200 are used for just one programme.

▲ Hand-held microphones are often used outside, where interviewers need to be able to move around.

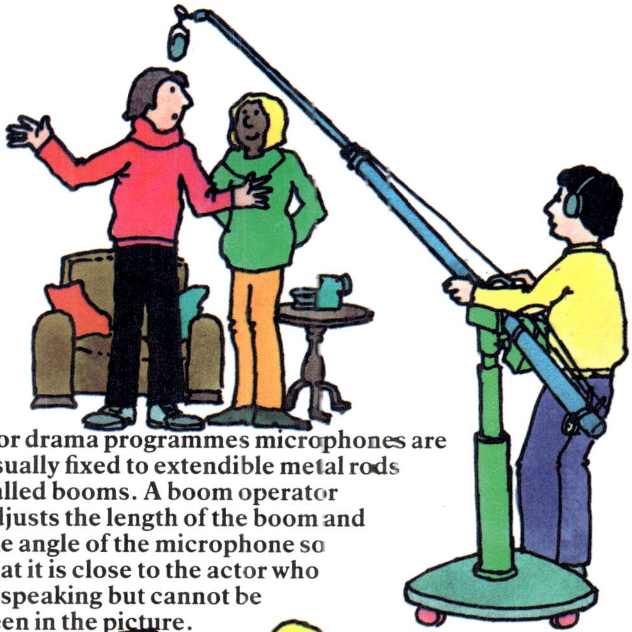

▲ For drama programmes microphones are usually fixed to extendible metal rods called booms. A boom operator adjusts the length of the boom and the angle of the microphone so that it is close to the actor who is speaking but cannot be seen in the picture.

▲ Musicians usually use microphones fixed to adjustable metal stands.

◄ Small microphones pinned to a piece of clothing are often used on chat shows.

Picking up the right sounds

One of the problems sound engineers have to cope with is how to pick up the sound they want without also picking up all sorts of sounds that they do not want. They do this by selecting and positioning microphones very carefully and by adjusting the distance from which they will pick up sound. Different microphones have different sensitivities to the sounds around them.

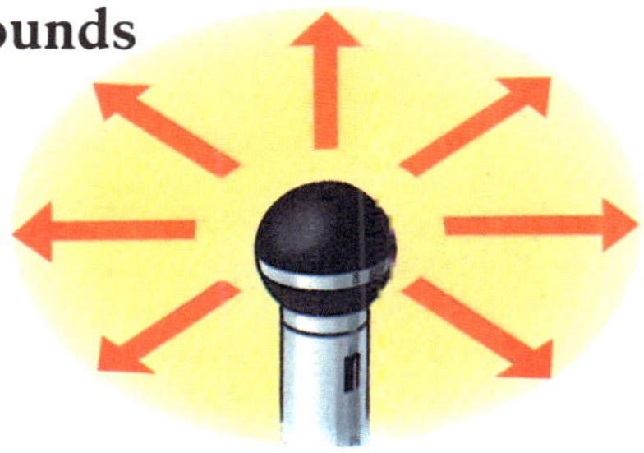

Some microphones pick up sounds equally from all directions. These are called omnidirectional or omnis for short.

A microphone that picks up sound only from the front and has a dead area behind it is called cardioid or directional.

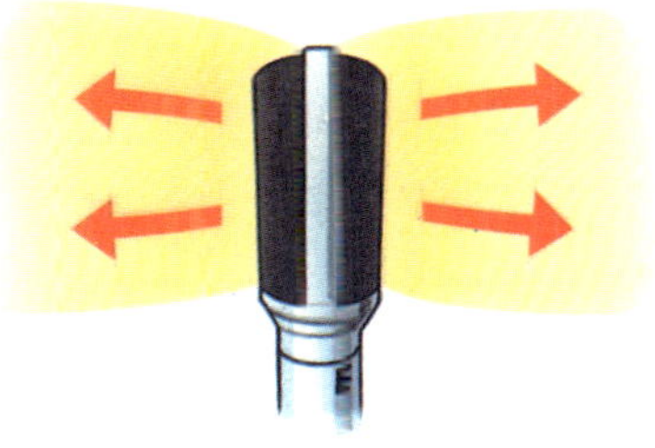

Some microphones pick up sound in a figure of eight area. These are bidirectional and are useful for two speakers facing one another.

How a microphone works

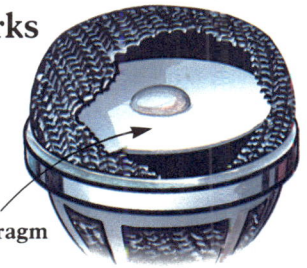
Diaphragm

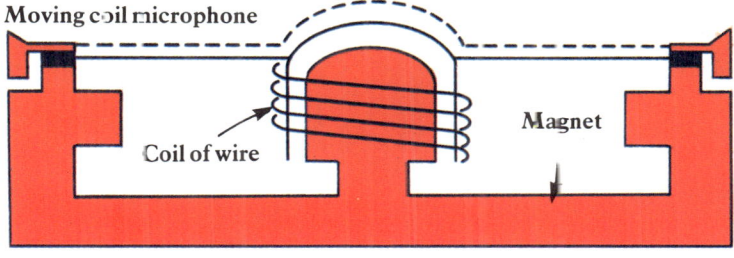
Moving coil microphone
Coil of wire
Magnet

Sound of any kind is caused by something vibrating. What we hear as sounds are vibrations inside our ears. Vibrations travel through the air and make other objects vibrate. The stronger the vibrations the louder the sound.

Inside a microphone is a very sensitive, metal plate called a diaphragm. Vibrations in the air, caused by sound, make it vibrate as well. The louder the sound the further it moves; the higher the sound the faster it moves.

Attached to the diaphragm is a device which turns its vibrations into electric signals. The devices for doing this give different microphones their names – "moving coil", "ribbon", "capacitor".

In a moving coil microphone there is a magnet and a thin coil of wire attached to the diaphragm. When a wire moves near a magnet an electric current begins to flow. This current becomes the sound signal.

In a TV studio

Most TV programmes are made inside TV studios. A television station or centre usually contains several studios of different sizes. Attached to each studio is a set of three control rooms: the sound control room, the lighting and vision control room and the production control room. A central control room coordinates all the programmes and links material broadcast by the station.

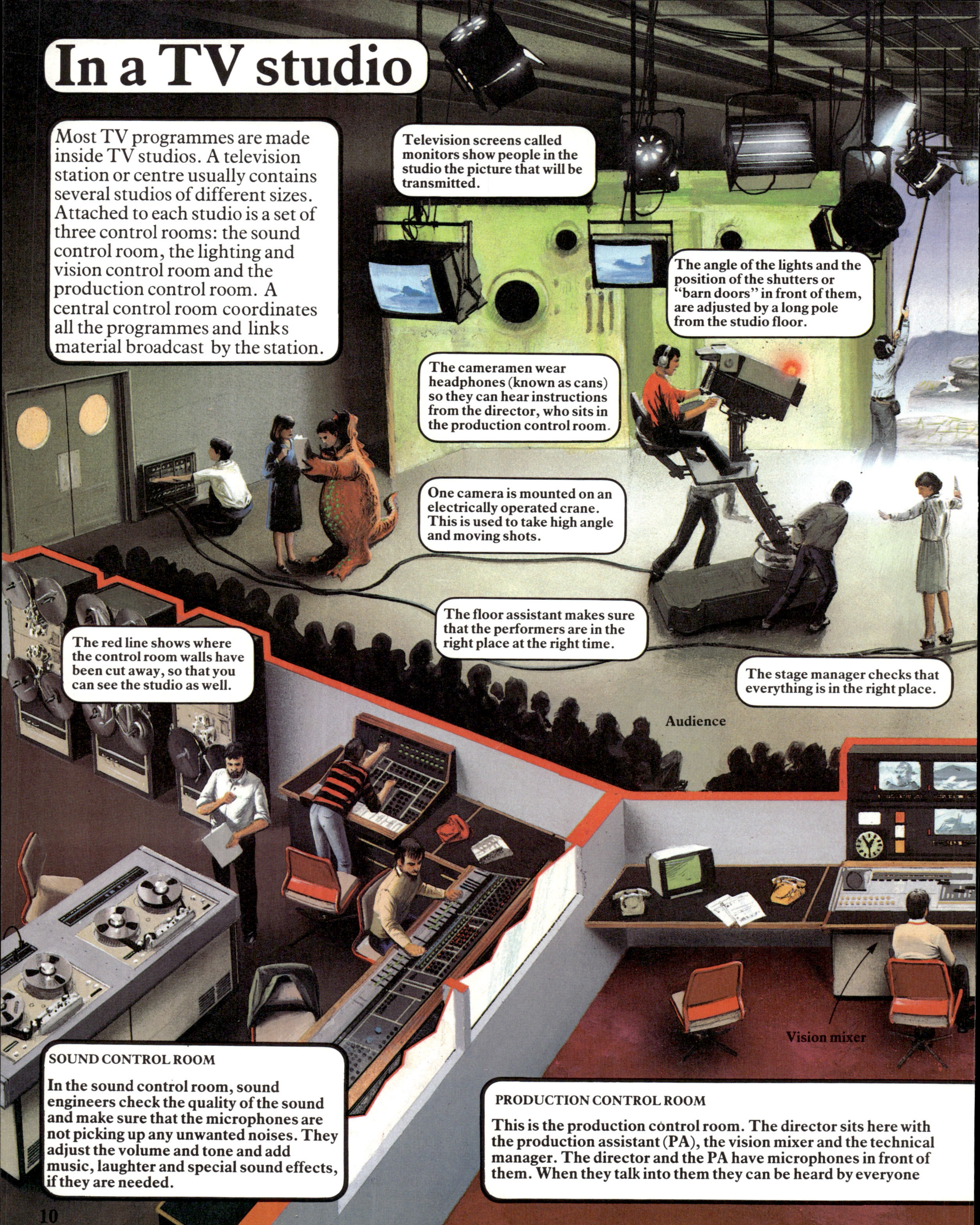

Television screens called monitors show people in the studio the picture that will be transmitted.

The angle of the lights and the position of the shutters or "barn doors" in front of them, are adjusted by a long pole from the studio floor.

The cameramen wear headphones (known as cans) so they can hear instructions from the director, who sits in the production control room.

One camera is mounted on an electrically operated crane. This is used to take high angle and moving shots.

The floor assistant makes sure that the performers are in the right place at the right time.

The red line shows where the control room walls have been cut away, so that you can see the studio as well.

The stage manager checks that everything is in the right place.

Audience

Vision mixer

SOUND CONTROL ROOM

In the sound control room, sound engineers check the quality of the sound and make sure that the microphones are not picking up any unwanted noises. They adjust the volume and tone and add music, laughter and special sound effects, if they are needed.

PRODUCTION CONTROL ROOM

This is the production control room. The director sits here with the production assistant (PA), the vision mixer and the technical manager. The director and the PA have microphones in front of them. When they talk into them they can be heard by everyone

The lights hang from a grid on the ceiling. Each one has a motor and can be moved up and down by touching a switch on the studio floor.

Microphone

TV stations vary a great deal in size. Some of them are just big rooms, others are more like cinemas or theatres with tiered seats for a studio audience. In this one an episode of a sci-fi series is being made.

There are several different sets in the studio. Each one has the background and props for a different part of the action.

There are also several cameras. Each one shoots the scene from a different angle. The electronic signals from the cameras pass down cables through the vision control room to the production room, where the director chooses which picture will actually be transmitted. The sound signals pass from the microphones in the studio through the sound control room to the production control room.

For drama programmes there would not be an audience in the studio. Audiences are only allowed in for certain programmes such as comedies and chat shows.

Actors

Sound boom

A small light on top of each camera shows which camera is taking the picture that will actually be transmitted.

The floor manager is the director's contact in the studio. He receives instructions through his headphones and makes sure that everything runs smoothly.

Director   PA   Technical manager

wearing headphones in the studio and the people in the sound and vision rooms. Pictures from the cameras appear on the TV screens in front of them. The director gives directions to the cameramen, the floor manager and the vision mixer. To find out more about the control room see pages 12 and 13.

VISION CONTROL ROOM

All vision signals from the cameras go through this room to the production control room. The vision controller checks the technical quality and colour balance of the picture. Also from here the lighting supervisor controls the position and brightness of the lights.

11

In the control room

This is the production control room of a news programme. It is being broadcast live so everyone has to think very quickly to make it all run smoothly without mistakes. The director looks at the pictures from various sources, which appear on the monitors (screens) and decides which one should be broadcast at any moment and when to switch to another one. He gives instructions to the vision mixer, who operates the knobs and switches to achieve what the director wants. The director can also talk to the cameramen and floor manager through their headphones. If he wants to talk to the newsreader he has to press a special key. This is so that the newsreader is not distracted by a stream of instructions to other people.

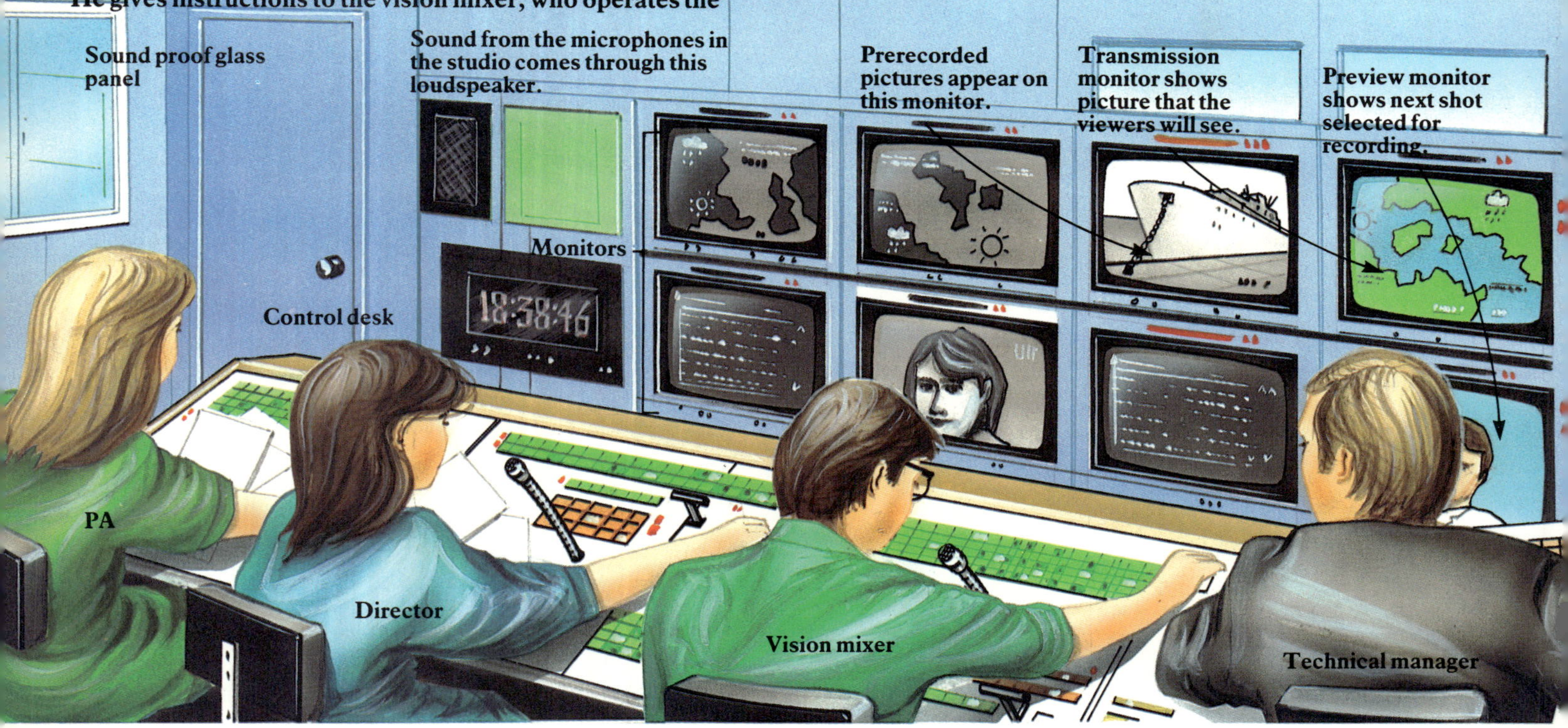

Sound proof glass panel

Sound from the microphones in the studio comes through this loudspeaker.

Prerecorded pictures appear on this monitor.

Transmission monitor shows picture that the viewers will see.

Preview monitor shows next shot selected for recording.

Control desk

Monitors

18:38:46

PA

Director

Vision mixer

Technical manager

Reading the news

The newsreader sits in a small studio near the production control room. He wears an earpiece through which he can hear instructions from the director.

A roll of paper with his words printed on it is fed across a table and past the lens of a small camera mounted above it. This machine is called a teleprompt. The picture taken by the teleprompt is fed to a small screen mounted at right angles below the camera lens, so that the newsreader can read his words while appearing to look directly at the camera. To the camera lens the words are invisible.

Any words, such as captions, titles or credits, that are to appear on the screen during the course of the programme are put on to an easel or loaded into a caption roller and placed in front of one of the cameras ready to be rolled past the lens. Machines called character generators* are, however, replacing caption rollers in many studios.

Teleprompter

Floor manager. He gives the newsreader his cues.

Caption roller

Monitor showing picture that is being transmitted.

Newsreader

*To find out more about these machines see page 25

The control desk

This is a close-up of the control panel from the production control room. The rows of buttons are known as buses. In each row across there is one button for each of the cameras and for each of the other sources, such as video tape machines, from which pictures are available.

If the vision mixer is cutting straight from one picture to another, he only needs to use one row of buttons. When he presses a button, it lights up showing that the picture from that camera is passing out of the desk to be transmitted.

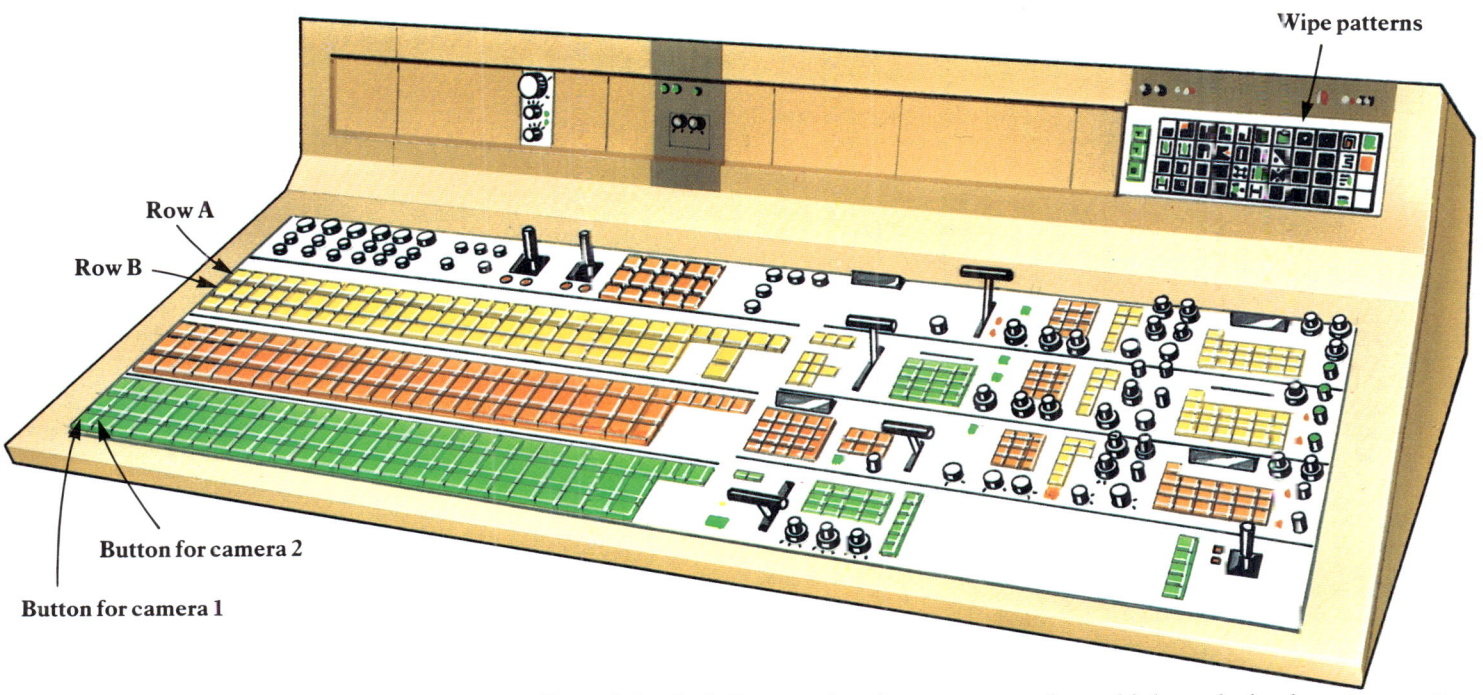

Row A
Row B
Button for camera 2
Button for camera 1
Wipe patterns

But the vision mixer can also mix (fade) one picture gradually into another. If he has selected camera 1 on row A and he wants to mix to camera 2, he presses the 2 button on row B and then moves the lever at the right slowly down. This has the effect of slowly fading out the picture from row A and slowly bringing in the picture from row B.

The change from one picture to another can also be done by a technique called wiping. This is when a moving edge, which can be in almost any pattern, leads the new picture across the screen, appearing to wipe the old one away. At the top of the panel a display of buttons shows some of the wipe patterns the vision mixer can select.

Cuts, mixes and wipes

Here you can see what cuts, mixes and wipes look like on the screen. These are the simplest ways of changing from one shot to another.

Cut

Mix

Wipe

Transmitting TV pictures

Most people receive the pictures on their TV sets through the air. Electric signals from cameras and microphones are sent along cables from the TV station to a transmitting station. There they are combined with radio waves and then sent out through the air to be received by aerials connected to TV sets in people's homes.

Sometimes underground cables are used to carry the signals. This happens particularly in places where there are special problems involved in transmitting signals through the air. To transmit programmes over very large distances, satellites are used. The use of both underground cables and satellites for transmission is increasing all the time.

Radio waves go out in all directions, rather like light from a lighthouse.

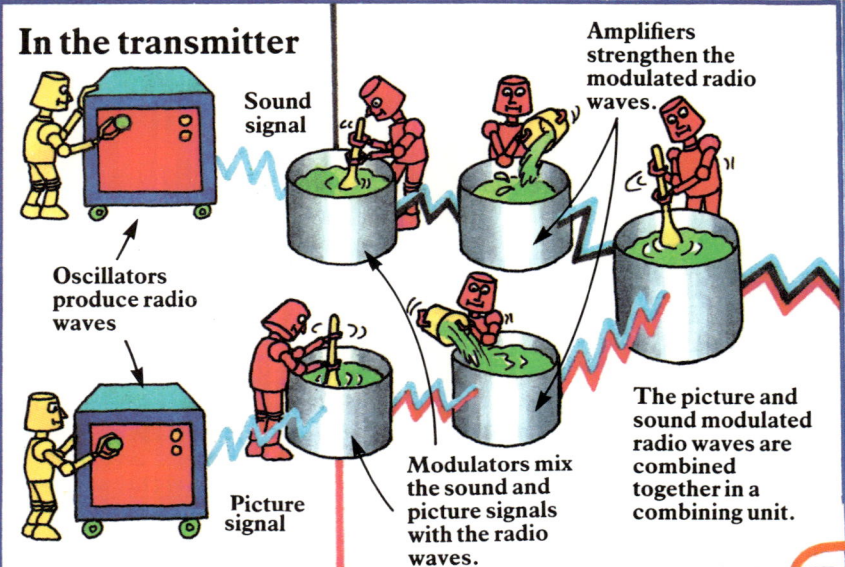

In the transmitter

Sound signal

Oscillators produce radio waves

Picture signal

Amplifiers strengthen the modulated radio waves.

Modulators mix the sound and picture signals with the radio waves.

The picture and sound modulated radio waves are combined together in a combining unit.

In the transmitter there are two "oscillators". These make two radio waves – one to carry the picture information and one to carry the sound information. The two radio waves are sent to two "modulators" where they are mixed with (or modulated by) the sound and vision signals. The modulated radio waves are then amplified (strengthened by amplifiers), combined together and fed to the transmitting aerials.

▲**The transmitting aerial sends out the radio waves in all directions. The type of radio waves used to carry signals are made very much weaker if they travel through solid objects, so transmitting aerials are usually positioned high up on hills, or tall buildings, so that the signals do not hit any obstructions.**

◄**The receiving aerial picks up the signal and sends it down a cable to the TV set.**

Radio waves

Long wave (low frequency)

Short wave (high frequency)

Radio waves are described either by their wavelength (the distance between the top of one wave and the top of the next) or by their frequency (the number of waves per second). Long waves have low frequencies, short waves have high frequencies. TV signals are usually transmitted on very high frequency (VHF) waves, or ultra high frequency (UHF) waves.

All TV companies broadcasting in one particular area must use a different wavelength to transmit their signals. If they used the same ones or ones that were too close together, the information would get jumbled together and the TV sets would not be able to sort them out.

Transmitting by radio waves

Radio waves from TV transmitters cannot usually travel much more than about 80km. To broadcast over larger distances TV companies need to have several transmitters to pick up the signal from each other and pass it on. Where there are mountains, which would obstruct the signal, it must be carried over, either by a transmitter on top or by a land line. People living near mountains sometimes receive the same signal twice – once direct from the transmitter and once after it has bounced off the mountain and back to their aerial. The result is "ghosting", a faint shadow picture to the side of the main picture. To avoid this problem a local relay station is sometimes built. It picks up the signal from the main transmitter and broadcasts it on a different wavelength. People having problems receiving the main signal can tune their sets to a different frequency.

1 Transmitting by satellite

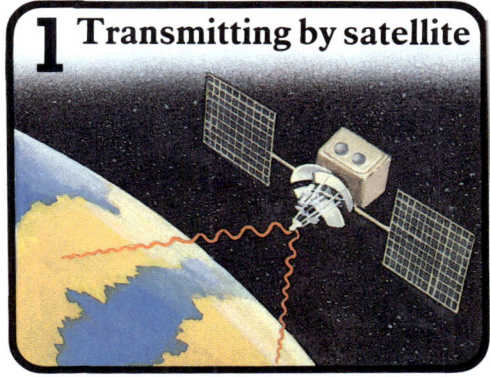

The best way of broadcasting over very large distances is to use a satellite circling several thousand kilometres above the earth's surface. Radio waves carrying TV signals are beamed up to it by a very powerful transmitter. When the satellite receives the signals it beams them back over a large area of the earth's surface.

2

The signal beamed back to earth by a satellite has to be picked up by a dish aerial. It can then be sent to viewers either by cable or by radio waves. As satellites capable of producing more and more powerful signals are developed, the dishes needed to receive the signals are becoming smaller and smaller.

3

The latest type of satellites are called Direct Broadcast Satellites. They give out such strong signals that they can be received by a dish aerial less than a metre in diameter – small enough to fit on the roof of a house, or in a small garden. The signal from the satellite can therefore go direct to individual homes.

1 Transmitting by cable

TV programmes are often sent from one country to another by underground cable and this system is also one solution for bad reception. A cable company puts up a high aerial and runs cables from it to customers who pay each month for the service.

The cables can carry a large number of different channels, but in most places only a few programmes are broadcast at any one time. So cable companies started offering programmes of their own. Some of them charge their customers more for each extra channel or certain special programmes.

2

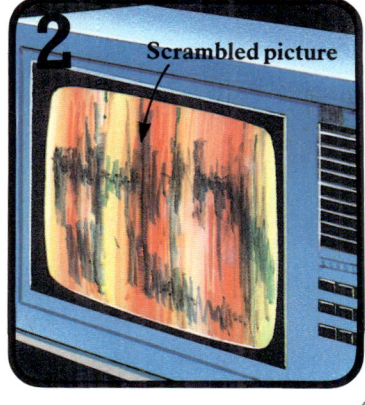

Scrambled picture

In early pay TV systems viewers had to put coins in a slot. In the latest systems central computers record which channels customers have paid for. Pictures are sent out "scrambled". A box beside each TV set "descrambles" the picture if the computer approves it.

3

The latest development in cable TV systems is the fibre optic cable. The signals are carried by a laser beam – a very powerful beam of light. This is passed down a thread of glass, no thicker than an ordinary light flex. These cables can carry several hundred channels at a time.

TV sets

The job of a TV set is to turn the electronic signals created by TV cameras and microphones back into pictures and sound. The aerial picks up the signals from the transmitting aerials and they then travel down a cable to the aerial socket at the back of the TV. When you switch on the set the sound and picture signals are separated from each other and from the carrier waves. The sound is sent to a loudspeaker. The picture signal is sent to the picture tube, which converts it into the picture you see.

1 Tricking the eyes

If you look closely at a TV screen, you can see that the picture is made up of lots of horizontal lines. In Europe and much of the rest of the world TV screens have 625 lines, in America and Japan they have 525.

2

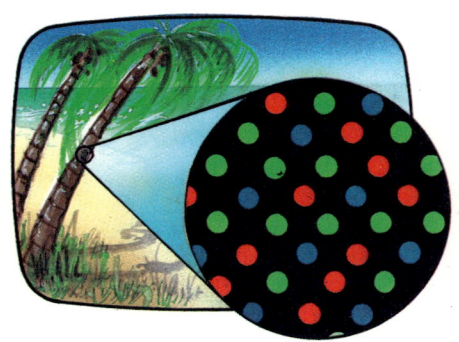

If you look even closer you will see that each line is made up of a series of red, green and blue dots (some TVs have strips instead of dots) of varying brightness. Most screens have over a million of these dots. The three colours mix in your eyes to produce all the colours you see on the screen.

How the picture tube works

The picture tube in a TV set works like the camera tube* in reverse. When the picture signal has been separated from the sound signal it is split into three separate signals – one red, one blue and one green. The tube converts these signals back into coloured light. The type shown here is called a shadow mask tube. There are other kinds but this is the most common.

The screen is the front part of the picture tube. On the inside it is covered with tiny dots of a chemical called phosphor. Three different types of phosphor are used. One type glows red when hit by electrons, one glows blue and one glows green.

At the back of the picture tube are three electron guns that fire beams of electrons at the screen. The amount of electricity leaving the guns is controlled by the three picture signals which are fed to the picture tube. A strong beam makes the phosphor glow brightly and a weak beam makes it glow dimly. The beams move across the back of the screen line by line.

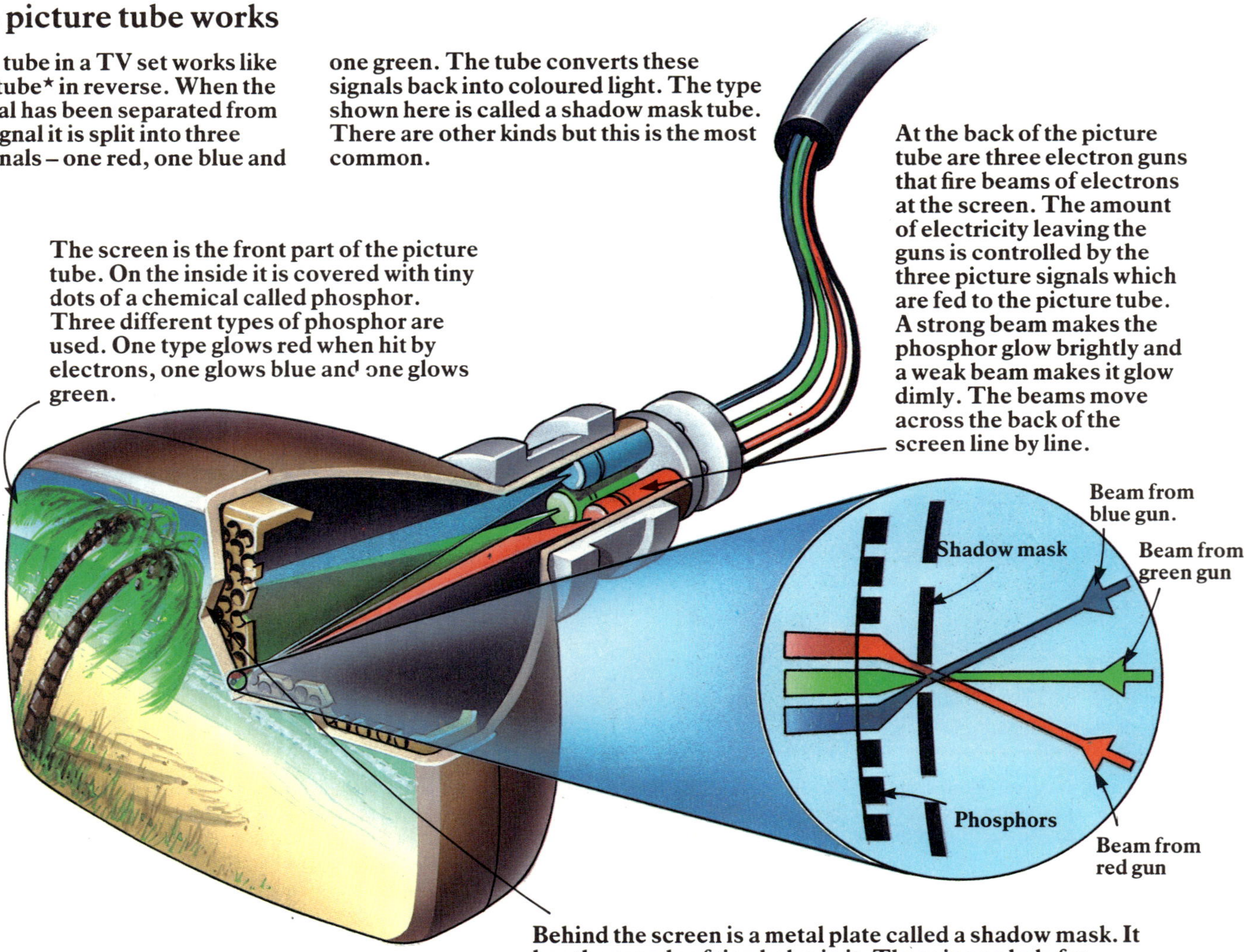

Beam from blue gun.

Shadow mask

Beam from green gun

Phosphors

Beam from red gun

Behind the screen is a metal plate called a shadow mask. It has thousands of tiny holes in it. There is one hole for every three dots of phosphor on the screen. The holes are positioned in such a way that each of the three electron beams can only strike the right type of phosphor.

3

The picture on the screen is actually created one dot at a time. Each dot in turn lights up and fades line by line down the screen. Any picture that the brain receives takes 1/10th of a second to fade away, but the dots light up and fade so quickly, that every dot on the screen appears to be lit all the time.

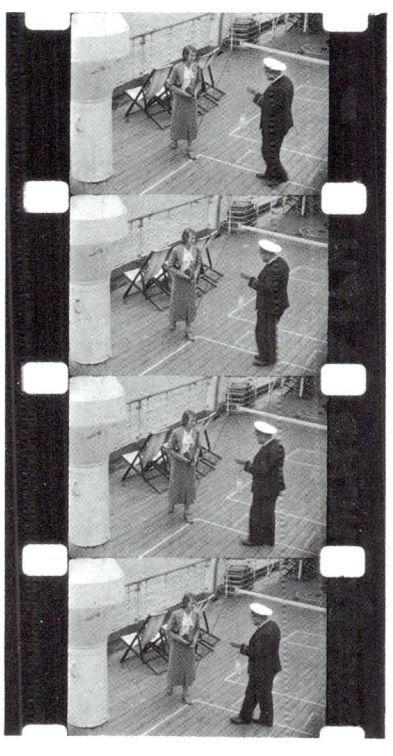

4

The slow-to-fade effect of human sight is called "persistence of vision". Cine films use this factor to create an impression of continuous movement. They are in fact a series of still photographs or "frames" taken in very quick succession – usually 24 frames per second. When they are projected at the same speed, our eyes see one continuous picture.

In TV systems that have 625 lines per frame TV frames are shown at the rate of 25 complete frames every second. This means that when films are shown on television they run fractionally faster than they would do in a cinema, but the difference is so small that you can hardly notice it.

Selecting a channel

Most TV sets offer a choice of programmes from several different broadcasting stations. The radio waves that carry the TV signals are divided into channels according to their wavelength and frequency.★ Within each area, each station is given a different channel, so that they will all be using different frequencies to transmit their signals. There are gaps between each channel to make sure the signals do not interfere with each other.

When the radio waves enter the TV set they pass into a tuner. The tuner will only allow waves within a certain band of frequencies to pass into the rest of the set. But the tuner is adjustable and can be altered to allow a different band of frequencies in. You adjust the tuner by turning a knob or pressing buttons on the front of the TV set. When you first get the set or you want to pick up a new broadcasting station the tuner has to be adjusted so that when you press one of the buttons or turn the knob it allows in the band of frequencies on which that station is broadcasting in your area. Each knob can be preset to any channel.

Remote controls

Some remote control units are attached to the television by an electric cable. Others have no cable and control the set by means of an invisible infra-red light beam. The beam carries instructions to the television in a light code, similar to morse code. Inside the TV there is a sensor which recognizes only infra-red light. It translates the beam from the light signal into electrical information. A decoder then sends the information to the right place in the TV set.

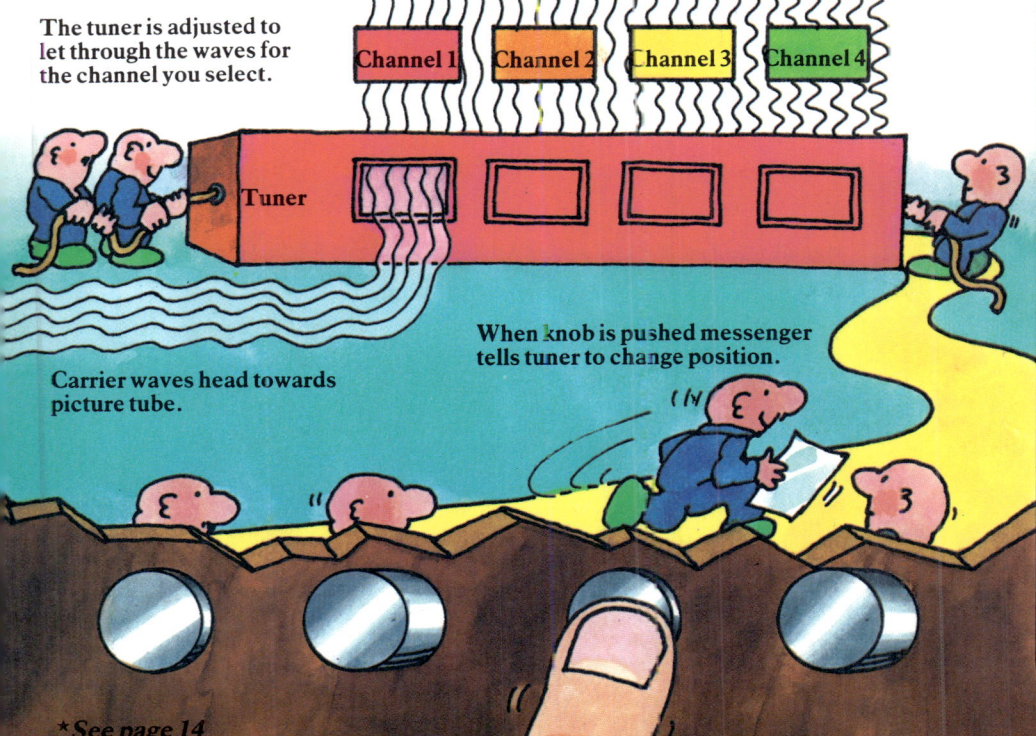

The tuner is adjusted to let through the waves for the channel you select.

Channel 1 Channel 2 Channel 3 Channel 4

Tuner

Carrier waves head towards picture tube.

When knob is pushed messenger tells tuner to change position.

Outside the studios

Programme makers often have to go outside their TV studios for the material they need. This presents different problems from those that arise in studio productions and they have to work out what equipment they will need to solve them. Film equipment is lighter and more manoeuvrable than normal studio equipment and in some situations this is very important. But film does have to go through more processes before it can be broadcast. Events that need to be covered by several cameras and broadcast live or almost immediately are covered by "outside broadcast" units. This means taking along TV cameras and a travelling control room with a team of people to operate the equipment. The development of much lighter electronic video equipment is, however, beginning to bring about great changes in the way outside material is gathered.

The centre of operations in an outside ▶ broadcast is the mobile control room (MCR). This is a large van which contains the equipment normally found in the production, sound and vision control rooms linked to a TV studio. All the pictures from the TV cameras are sent back here and the ones selected for broadcasting are then sent back to the TV station by radio waves or by cables.

Outside broadcasts

Most sports programmes and other events not staged specially for the TV cameras are outside broadcasts (usually referred to as "*Oh bees*") and parts of other programmes are made in this way too. The location need not necessarily be outdoors. O.B.'s are often broadcast from theatres, concert halls and other indoor locations.

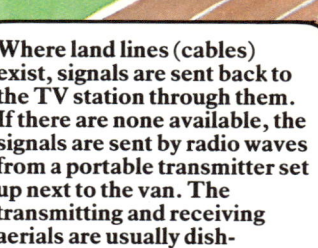

Commentators usually have a position overlooking the whole scene, but they also have monitors showing the pictures from each camera. They base their commentary partly on what they can actually see and partly on the monitors, so that can fit their commentary to what the viewer can see.

Where land lines (cables) exist, signals are sent back to the TV station through them. If there are none available, the signals are sent by radio waves from a portable transmitter set up next to the van. The transmitting and receiving aerials are usually dish-shaped.

Production control area

Sound engineer

Vision engineer

Gun microphone

Camera 1

Camera and microphone cables plug in here.

1 News gathering

Speed is vitally important when gathering news stories. Until quite recently most news pictures were obtained on film. Small two-man film crews can get to scenes of action very quickly, taking all their equipment in one van or car.

2

Once the film has been shot it has to be taken back to the studio as fast as possible. A motorbike messenger is often used. In the TV station it has to be developed, edited and put through a telecine machine before it is ready to be transmitted.

3

Now that smaller and lighter cameras and video tape equipment have been developed, a two-man TV camera team can also get news pictures without taking a lot of cumbersome equipment with them. This is called electronic news gathering (ENG).

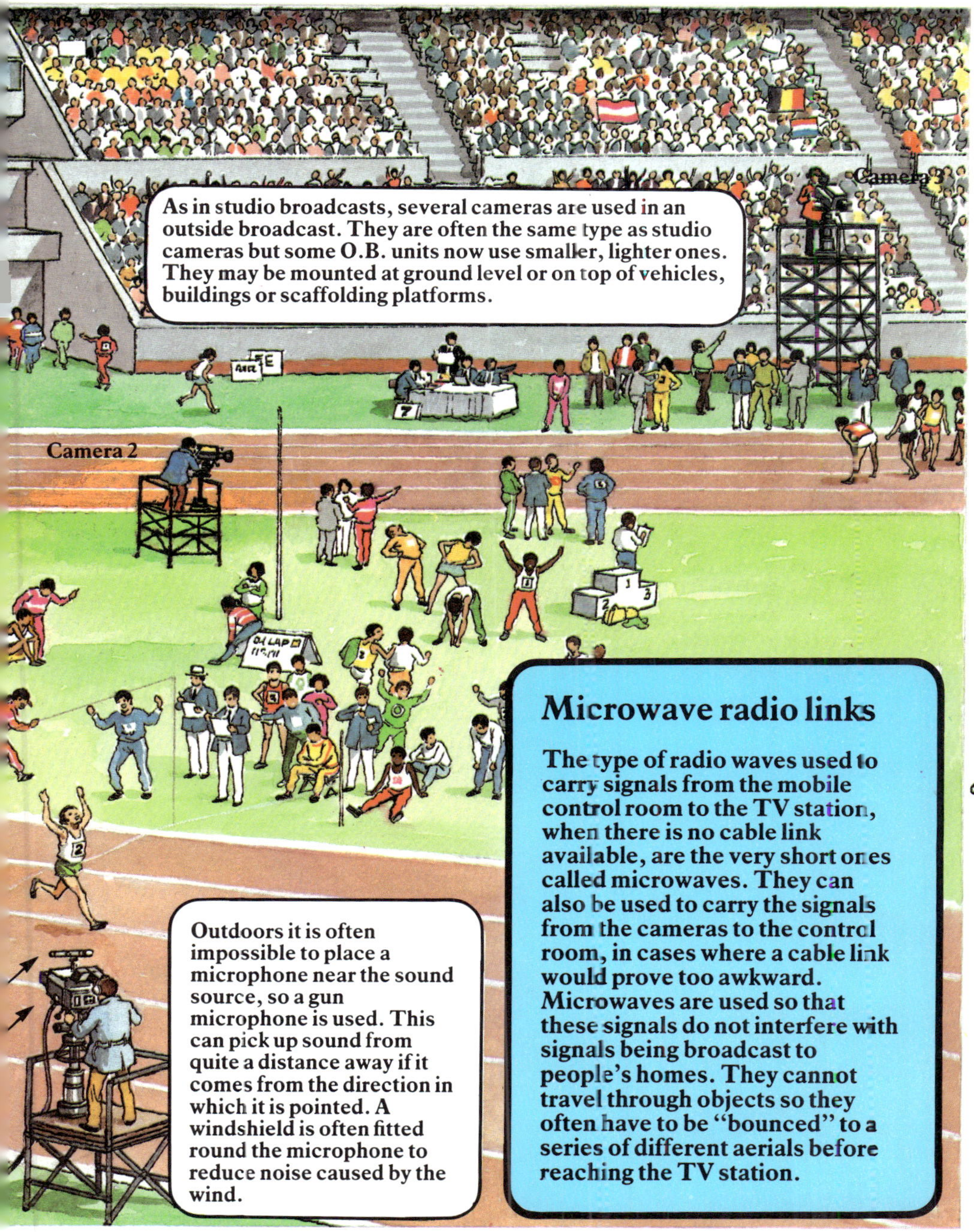

As in studio broadcasts, several cameras are used in an outside broadcast. They are often the same type as studio cameras but some O.B. units now use smaller, lighter ones. They may be mounted at ground level or on top of vehicles, buildings or scaffolding platforms.

Camera 3

Camera 2

Outdoors it is often impossible to place a microphone near the sound source, so a gun microphone is used. This can pick up sound from quite a distance away if it comes from the direction in which it is pointed. A windshield is often fitted round the microphone to reduce noise caused by the wind.

Microwave radio links

The type of radio waves used to carry signals from the mobile control room to the TV station, when there is no cable link available, are the very short ones called microwaves. They can also be used to carry the signals from the cameras to the control room, in cases where a cable link would prove too awkward. Microwaves are used so that these signals do not interfere with signals being broadcast to people's homes. They cannot travel through objects so they often have to be "bounced" to a series of different aerials before reaching the TV station.

Filming on location

When programme makers decide to use film cameras for shots outside the studios, this is called filming on location. Many drama programmes contain filmed sequences. The location may not be outdoors. Often it is very hard to make shots in a studio look realistic and it may be cheaper to use an existing building to get the right kind of atmosphere and detail.

Cameraman

Assistant cameraman

Sound recordist

PA

Director

One camera is used and each shot is carefully planned and prepared in advance. The sound and pictures are recorded separately. The clapperboard is used at the beginning of each shot, so that the sound and the picture can be exactly matched, or synchronized, when they are put together.

Electronic field production

The newer, lightweight electronic equipment is now beginning to be used for some drama programmes where film would previously have been used. This way of working is rather similar to the procedure in making home videos.

4

The tape can be taken back to the TV station by a messenger, but it is also possible to send the pictures by land line or by microwave radio link. The crew often travel in vans with a microwave transmitter on top. At the station the pictures can be transmitted instantly.

5

Some of the latest cameras now have a compact video cassette recorder built into the main body of the camera. This makes it possible for one person to record pictures and sound and send them back to the station.

Recording and editing

Most programmes are recorded and edited before being transmitted. Sometimes film is used but more often they are recorded on video tape.

For sound recording the tape width is ¼ or ⅛ of an inch. In video recording there is much more information to store. In TV broadcasting 2 inch or 1 inch tape is used. Tapes for use in industry are ¾ inch and cassettes for home use are ½ an inch. There are also now ¼ inch video tapes for use in some portable video recorders.

▲ Video tape recorders (VTRs) are used for both recording and editing tape. They are the professional version of the domestic video cassette recorder (VCR). The tape is on large reels instead of cassettes.

How an electronic signal is recorded on tape

To record a sound or vision signal on tape, the electronic signal must first be converted into a magnetic signal. This is done by a recording head.

When the tape is rewound and played back the recording head "reads" the magnetic pattern and converts it back into an electronic signal.

Recording head

The unrecorded tape is fed to the recording head. the tape is made of plastic coated with a layer of tiny particles of iron oxide. As it passes across the recording head the particles of iron oxide are magnetized by the iron block. Their magnetic strength varies with the magnetic strength of the block at the moment they pass across it. In this way the signal is stored on the tape in the form of a magnetic pattern.

A recording head consists of a coil of wire wrapped around a small block of iron. When the signal reaches the wire the iron block becomes magnetized. Its magnetic strength varies with the strength of the electronic signal.

Moving heads

In sound recording the sound is recorded in straight lines down the length of the tape and the recording head does not move as the tape moves past it. For video recording, ways had to be developed of packing a much greater volume of information on to the tape in a more economical fashion. If the sound recording system were used for video recording you would need more than 100km of tape to record a one hour programme.

To overcome this problem the recording heads on video tape recorders move as the tape moves past them. By laying the information across the tape they fit more of it into the same amount of space.

Sound is laid down this edge of the tape.

Head drum

Tracks

Head

The heads protrude through a slit in the drum.

In VCRs and the newer VTRs used in broadcasting a "helical" (spiral) system of moving recording heads is used. Two, sometimes four, heads are mounted on a wheel inside a drum. The tape wraps round the drum in a spiral path and, as it slides across the drum, the wheel with the heads rotates in the opposite direction. The information is laid on the tape in long, slanting tracks. Sound is transferred to a strip down one edge of the tape by a separate sound recording head.

Editing

Editing is the process of assembling a series of different scenes or "shots" into one continuous programme. It involves cutting out certain shots, or parts of them, and changing the sequence of others. The editor may need to cut the overall length of a programme, or to cut out mistakes and retakes. The impression each shot makes on the viewer can be completely altered by cutting out a few frames.

Film editing

Film editing

Electronic editing

Video tape editing is done by dubbing (copying) material from one tape on to another. At least two machines are used – one to playback the first tape and one to record the selected pieces from the first tape on to the second tape.

Editing requires split second timing. In TV stations editing suites, like the one shown here, usually use computers to control the process. This helps to ensure

that the joins are made in the exact place chosen by the editor and director.

You cannot edit videotape by cutting it up and joining together the pieces you want. This is partly because you cannot see the images on the tape so it would be very difficult to know exactly where to cut, but also because cutting tape creates enormous picture disturbance and joins can damage the recording heads.

In film editing you can actually see the image on each frame of the film. The editor cuts the film and joins the selected pieces together with transparent tape. To find shots quickly all the bits of film are carefully filed in cans. The room where film editing is done is called the cutting room.

Editing at home

To edit tapes at home you need two video cassette recorders connected to each other by the video out/in and audio out/in sockets. It helps if you also use two TV sets, but you could make do with one.

First view your tape and decide which sections you want to use and in what order. Use the tape counter to help you remember. Then record the sections in the selected order by playing them on VCR 1 and putting VCR 2 on record.

The aim is to get the joins as invisible as possible. If VCR 2 has an edit start button it will help to cut down picture distortion. It also helps if tape 1 is already running when you start to record on tape 2. Start tape 1 a little before the section you want and use the pause control on VCR 2 to bring in tape 2 at exactly the right moment. The quality of the picture will be a little worse on tape 2 than on the original.

Use this to see what you are recording.

Check what you have recorded on this.

VCR 1

VCR 2

Special electronic effects

The picture that appears on your TV screen is not always exactly like the live scene originally taken by the camera. The camera can only take what it sees, but in the control room or editing suite the image from one camera can be electronically combined with other images. Combinations of different images in one picture can be used to create very strange and magical effects, but they can also produce the kind of results we have become used to seeing on news and current affairs programmes. These two pages explain how some of the effects are produced. When you are watching TV see if you can tell which technique has been used.

1 Double shots

One of the effects that modern recording methods can achieve is a double shot. An actor (Fred One) can appear on the screen with himself (Fred Two) as though he were two separate people. He can even carry on a conversation with himself.

First the actor plays the part of Fred One. He has to be careful to keep to the left of the set and to leave pauses long enough for Fred Two's replies. The scene is recorded on video tape A and the tape is then rewound.

Chromakey

Chromakey is the most common technique used for combining two pictures. It can be used to show a map or photo behind a newscaster or presenter, or to show more fantastic and magical scenes.

Chromakey works by cutting out all parts of a picture that are in one "key" colour. A bright blue is usually chosen as the key colour. In the picture above, the newsreader sits in front of a blue background. The camera's output is passed through an electronic switch. As each line of the scene reaches it, the switch checks whether it is blue or not. Wherever it finds a patch of blue, it rejects it and switches instead to another source. The programme director can choose any other source. Here he has chosen camera 2, which is focused on a map, but he could choose a picture from an outside broadcast or satellite relay from another part of the world. The newscaster must be careful not to wear anything blue, because if he does, part of his body will seem to disappear.

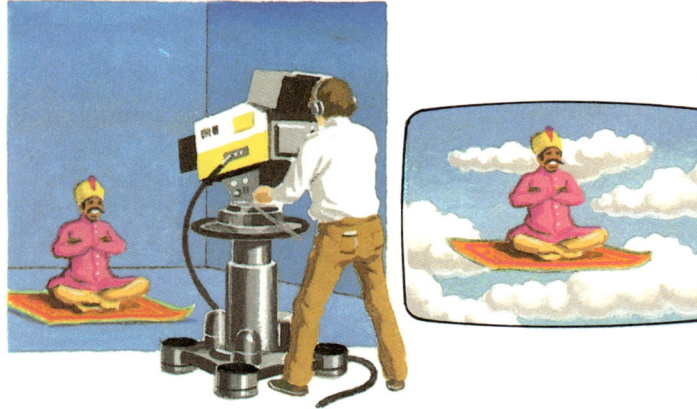

For a flying carpet scene, the carpet can be laid out on a floor which has been painted blue. The camera must look down on the scene so that all the background colour is blue. The background can come from film of the sky taken from an aeroplane.

The switch can be adjusted so that instead of rejecting the key colour, it lets through only the key colour. By using this technique the background can be made to remain, while figures, or other foreground shapes disappear, leaving only their outlines. The outlines can then be filled in by shots from another source.

3

Fred Two

The camera then shoots the same actor, now playing the part of Fred Two. This time he is careful to keep to the right-hand side of the set and to leave pauses for Fred One's parts of the conversation. The background must exactly match the first shot.

4

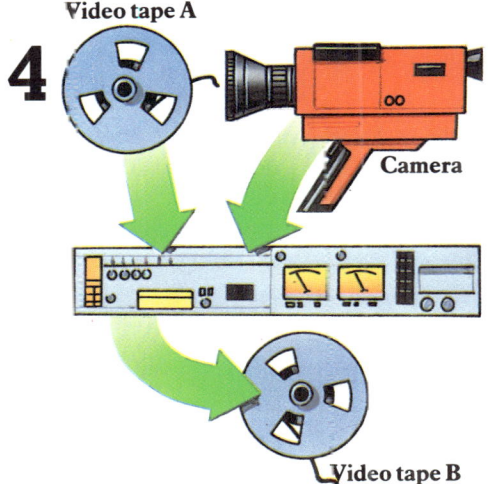

Video tape A

Camera

Video tape B

The signal from video tape A is sent to the mixing desk at the same time as the shot of Fred Two. In the desk the left side of the tape shot and the right side of the camera shot are taken and combined together and recorded in the final version on tape B.

Painting by numbers

One simple electronic effect can imitate the appearance of a picture done by "painting by numbers" and give the picture on the screen a cartoon-like effect. This is done by using a switch, like the one used for chromakey, which can respond to a number of different levels of brightness in the picture. Each level of brightness can then be replaced by a different colour.

4

Chromakey can also be used to distort the scale of things in a scene. Here a timid man is scared by a giant cat. To achieve this effect camera 1 shoots a

close-up of the cat against a blue background. Camera 2 shoots the man from quite a distance away. Shot 2 is then fed into the blue parts of shot 1.

5

It is also possible to use chromakey to make someone disappear from the screen. The figure is keyed in from a second camera. You can then slowly mix

from the composite shot to the background alone with the effect that the figure appears to vanish.

Double shot with chromakey

The techniques used to show two life-sized Freds can be combined with the chromakey scale-distorting effect so that Fred Two appears to be a pin-sized man, dancing in the hand of Fred One. On the second recording Fred Two is photographed from far away against a blue background and overlayed on a prerecorded image of Fred One. The cameraman has to be careful to line up the feet of Fred Two so that he appears to be in the hand of Fred One.

Digital effects

Some very spectacular effects can be achieved on the TV screen by changing the shape and size of one or more picture frames. This is done by feeding the signal from the TV camera through a special computer. The signal from the camera is electronic and has to be converted into a number code before it can be processed by the computer. A signal based on numbers is called a digital signal, so special effects created by this method are called digital effects.

Here are some of the effects you can see on television which are achieved by using digital signals. See how many of them you can spot when watching TV.

A digital effects machine

The computer which changes the size and shape of the picture is known as a digital effects device. It is a large box inside which there are several boards with silicon chips attached to them.

Signal from TV camera

ANALOGUE-DIGITAL CONVERTER

The analogue signal from the TV camera enters the machine here. The first thing that happens inside the machine is that it is converted into a digital signal. This is done by testing it at regular intervals thousands of times a second. The strength of the signal at each point tested is interpreted as a number.

10.25

Instructions from operator arrive here.

CENTRAL PROCESSING UNIT

Instructions from the operator are fed straight into this section, which decides mathematically how to use the information in the store to create the effect the operator wants. It has just received the instruction "reduce the size of this picture to one quarter its present size".

Analogue and digital signals

The normal signal used in television is an electric current generated by light falling on the target plate of a camera tube and is called an "analogue" signal. It is a continuous signal and its strength varies in exact proportion to the strength of the light falling on the target plate.

Analogue signal

A digital signal is a series of electric pulses. The pulses form a number code. The strength of the light at any given point is represented by a number.

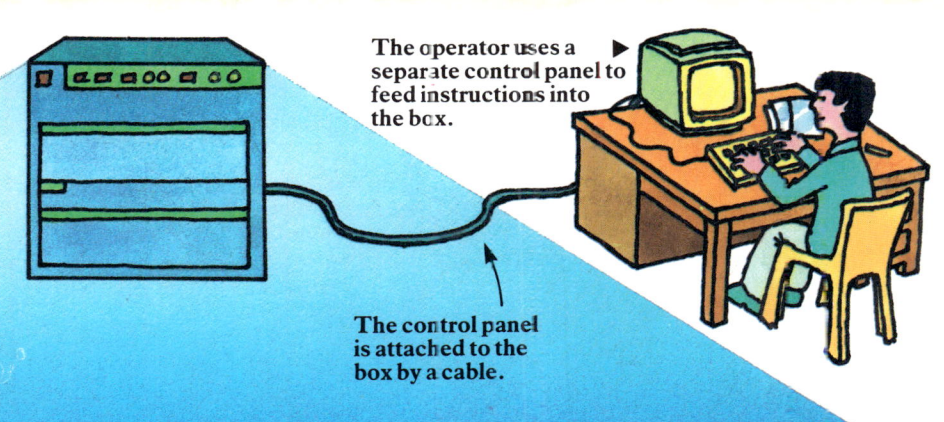

The operator uses a separate control panel to feed instructions into the box.

The control panel is attached to the box by a cable.

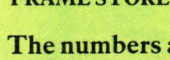

FRAME STORE

The numbers are carried in the form of electric pulses to the frame store. The frame store can only hold information about one complete picture frame at any one time. As soon as this information is taken out of the store and used, it starts filling up with information about another frame.

CLOCK

The clock is a vitally important part of the machine. All the stages described here take only thousandths of a second to happen, so the timing has to be extremely accurate.

Messages are sent to the frame store to tell it to send out one quarter of the numbers it has stored – each alternate number from each alternate line. These numbers are sent to the fourth department – the digital-analogue converter.

DIGITAL-ANALOGUE CONVERTER

Here the information about the quarter-size picture is translated from a digital signal back into an analogue signal, which can be carried by cables and transmitted to people's TV sets in the normal way.

Character generators

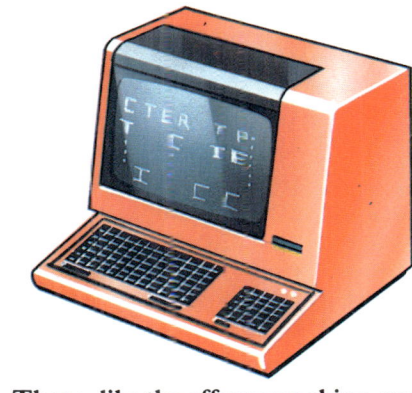

These, like the effects machine, are digital devices that allow letters, numbers and symbols to be typed into a keyboard and appear straight away on the TV screen. The information can be moved about the screen, flashed on and off, or rolled up to look like a roller caption.

Digital paint boxes

When you draw or write on the tablet of a digital paint box the result appears directly on the TV screen. The tablet responds to pressure by producing an electronic signal. The width and texture of the lines can be changed and you can fill in solid areas with colour.

Frame libraries

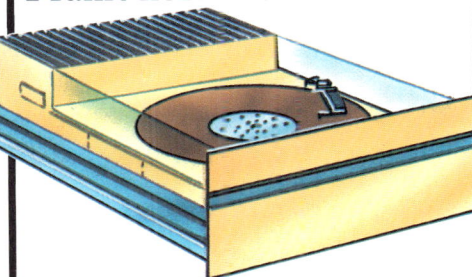

Using a computer disc for storing information, it is possible to file away hundreds of still TV frames. This means that a whole library can be built up from pictures frozen and grabbed from the TV, or from slides. These can be retrieved instantly and slotted into a programme.

TV and computers

The rapid progress of computer technology over the last few years, and particularly the development of home computers, is turning the TV set into a multi-purpose home terminal, linking you into all kinds of information systems other than just broadcast programmes. On these two pages are some of the computer uses of TV which are already in operation and some which are possible and likely to be used before too long.

There are lots of different ways of putting information into a computer, and of getting results from it. One of the ways a computer can display its results is by showing words, diagrams or graphs on a screen called a visual display unit (VDU) or monitor. A TV screen can serve as a display screen for a computer. The information is sent to the TV in the same form as a broadcast signal. It is then sent to the electron gun, which transfers the information to the screen.

Home computers

There is now a wide range of small computers available for home use. They can be used for playing games, for storing information, for making calculations and for learning how to do things. Home computers are designed for use with an ordinary TV set, which acts as its display screen, though you can also buy specially designed monitor screens. The computer itself comes in the form of a keyboard unit which has letters and numbers, like a typewriter, and also a set of instruction keys. The keyboard connects to the TV by a lead which plugs into the aerial socket.

Some computers are capable of producing colour on the screen and some will also produce sound.

TV games

A TV games system consists of a small computer, called a console, and a set of hand controls – usually joysticks, paddles or pressure pads. The console plugs into the aerial socket of your TV. The information the console needs to play each different game is contained on a silicon chip. Each chip contains about ten variations of the same game.

There are two types of TV games systems. In the first the games chip is fixed permanently in the console. In the second type you buy the games chips separately. They come inside plastic cartridges, which slot into the console. The more expensive the game you buy, the more sophisticated the display becomes and the more control you have over what happens on the screen. As time goes by the gap between TV games systems and home computers is gradually closing. Some of the newer systems provide you with a keyboard to put in your own games programs as well as using preprogrammed chips.

Computer information banks

TV sets can already be used to receive information coming from a central computer information bank outside your home. They are likely to be used more and more for this in the future.

The information can be sent to the TV in two different ways. It can be transmitted along with the normal TV signal and picked up by the TV aerial, though the TV set has to be specially adapted to receive it. This system is called teletext. The other system, called videotex, or viewdata, sends the information as signals along telephone wires. They have to be decoded in a special unit, called a modem, before the TV can understand them.

Both systems display screenfuls of the latest information on all kinds of subjects, including news, sport, weather, travel, finance and business. It is like having an instantly updated newspaper or magazine.

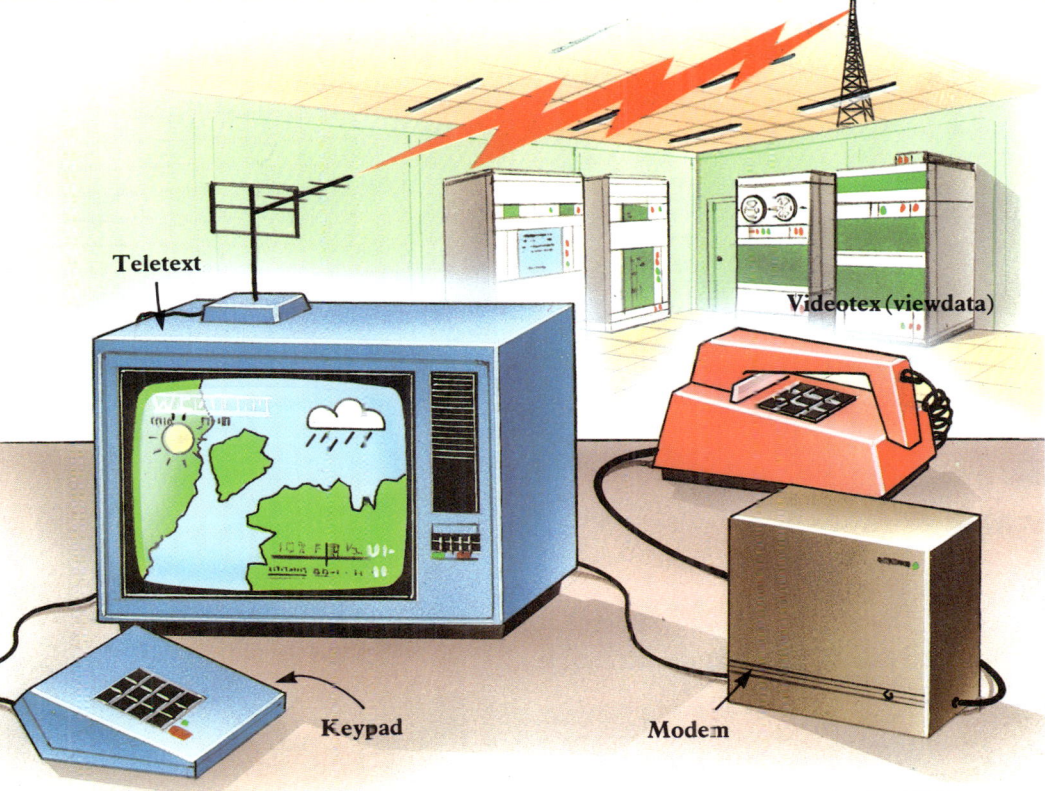

Teletext

Videotex (viewdata)

Keypad

Modem

Transmitting programs

To make a computer do anything you have to feed in a list of instructions and information, called a program. Instead of transmitting pages of straightforward factual information, the central computer could transmit pages of computer programs for use on home computers. The program could even be stored for later use on an audio tape cassette or a floppy disc linked up to the computer.

Interactive TV

WHICH ONE WOULD YOU VOTE FOR? A B C

Various systems of "talking back" to the TV set have been tested in different parts of the world. Viewers are provided with a keyboard and second screen. Questions come up on the second screen and information passes from the keyboard, via the telephone lines to a central computer in the TV studio. This system can be used for testing audience reaction to programmes, taking opinion polls and playing games.

Teleshopping

HALF PRICE SALE
NOW ONLY 99·99

In the future people may do much of their shopping by watching television. A TV in the home could be linked via a home computer to a computer in a shop. Goods from the shop would appear on the screen and you could use your computer to send orders to the shop's computer. It would give instructions to send you the goods and a bill.

Telebanking

BALANCE OF ACCOUNT
–258
PLEASE PAY IMMEDIATELY

There are already systems which allow you to call up your bank statement direct from the bank's information centre, if you have the right equipment. This could be extended to cover all your transactions with your bank. You could transfer funds and pay bills by typing instructions on a keyboard.

Teledoctor

HOW LONG HAVE YOU BEEN FEELING SICK?

Experiments have been made in diagnosing illnesses by using computers and the results have been surprisingly accurate. This could be developed so that if you felt ill you could call up a program on your screen, which would ask you a series of questions and then tell you what course of action to take.

Home video equipment

The development of electronic cameras and recorders which are small and cheap enough for people to have in their homes, is bringing about a revolution in home entertainment.

The central piece of equipment in the video revolution up to now is the video cassette recorder (VCR). The number of homes with a VCR increases rapidly month by month, as does the range of prerecorded cassettes to play on them.

While the recorder by itself gives you a much greater choice of viewing, used with a camera it provides a new leisure activity – creating your own TV programmes.

1 Video cassette recorders

A VCR is the domestic version of the video tape recorder used in TV broadcasting. The tapes are stored in handy cassettes instead of large reels. The lead from the TV aerial plugs into the aerial socket at the back of the VCR and a lead connects it to the TV set. The TV signal passes from the aerial to the VCR.

To record a programme the signal is then transferred to tape by the recording heads of the VCR. The TV does not even have to be switched on. To watch broadcast programmes at the time they are broadcast, the signal comes from the aerial, through the VCR to the TV.

3 VCR features

REWIND: Some machines will automatically rewind the tape when it reaches the end or the end of a programmed recording.

LOADER: This is where you put the cassette in. Some machines load from the front, some from the top. In top loaders you push the cassette into an open drawer and push the drawer down into the machine. Front loaders used motorized loading. The loader grabs the cassette from you and takes it down into the machine.

AUTOMATIC EDIT START: This gives you invisible joins between picture frames when you stop and start the tape. Very useful when you are recording from a camera.

FREEZE-FRAME (STILL FRAME): This allows you to hold a single frame continuously on the screen so that you can view it more closely. On most machines the picture quality is not very good on freeze.

FAST PICTURE SEARCH (FORWARDS AND BACKWARDS): This allows you to run through the tape very quickly (usually about five times the normal speed) while still keeping a picture on the screen. This is very useful for finding the beginning of recordings, missing out commercials and running through boring bits.

SLOW MOTION: Some machines have single speed others have variable speed – you slow the picture down gradually until it reaches the speed you want.

FAST PLAY/DOUBLE SPEED: This usually runs at two or three times the normal speed. It can be used for comic effect or for getting the messages from a programme very quickly.

FRAME BY FRAME/FRAME ADVANCE: You can advance the picture one frame at a time.

AUDIO DUB: This allows you to record sound on a previously recorded cassette, so that you replace the existing sound track. Only really useful if you are going to use a camera with your VCR.

TAPE COUNTER: You set the counter to 0 at the beginning of the tape. You can then use it to help you index your tape and find programmes quickly.

All VCRs allow you to record off the TV while you are watching the programme you want to record, while you are watching another channel, or while the TV is turned off. They have their own tuners built into them, which are completely separate from the tuner which selects the channels on the TV. They also have a timer, which you can set in advance to record at least one programme while you are out.

To do all these things all VCRs have certain basic "features". The more expensive the machine the more special features it has. Here you can see the main features that are available. The symbols used on the machines vary from one model to another.

2 VCR formats

There are three main types of VCR – VHS (Video Home System), Betamax and Video 2000 (the Philips system). Within each of these three formats there is a range of models at different prices and offering different facilities.

All three systems use half inch wide tape in their cassettes, but you cannot use cassettes made for one system on machines from either of the other two systems.

There are good machines in all three formats. In deciding which one to choose remember that to swap tapes with friends you must have the same format. It is also a good idea to check which prerecorded programmes are available in the format you have chosen.

Cameras and portable VCRs

With a video camera†you can record pictures and sound on to a cassette in your VCR. If the VCR is connected to a TV you can watch the picture on the screen, while recording it. The camera is linked to the VCR by a long lead. Sometimes you need to use an adaptor between them. If you want to record outside or have more freedom of movement, you need a portable VCR. These will work off batteries as well as mains electricity. You need a separate tuner if you also want to use your portable VCR to record broadcast programmes. A battery charger is very useful and will also act as a mains adaptor.

Portable VCR

Tuner →

Video discs

Video discs are similar to long playing records in size and shape. They are much cheaper to make than video tapes, but they cannot be used for home recording, either from the TV or from a camera. All you can do with a video disc player is play prerecorded discs. However, information can be stored and located very accurately on discs. This means that the quality of the picture is usually very good at all speeds. At the moment it seems likely that discs will be used more for business and educational purposes than for home entertainment.

As with VCRs there are different disc systems and each system uses a different type of disc.

CHANNEL SELECTOR: You select the TV channel you want by pressing these buttons. Some VCRs have the facility to receive up to 16 TV stations.

TAPE END ALARM: Light warns you when the tape is nearly finished.

CAMERA CONNECTOR: Some machines allow you to plug a lead from a camera straight into the VCR. With other machines you have to use a special adaptor or power supply unit.

CLOCK/TIMER DISPLAY PANEL: The clock shows the actual time. The timer is like an alarm which you set in advance to start the machine when the programme you want to record begins. When you set the timer, the clock disappears and the panel shows the day, time, channel and length of the programme you want to record.

The amount of time in advance you can set your machine to record varies between 12 hours and two or three weeks. "Programmable" or "multi-mode" timers allow you to preset your machine to record several different programmes at different times on different channels in advance (but remember that the tape playing time is usually only 3 or 4 hours).

4 Remote controls

Most VCRs now come with remote controls. The cheaper machines have a lead linking them to the remote controls. The more expensive use infra-red rays.★ Some just have a pause control, others have all the controls that are on the machine. Most people find that they do not use their trick frame facilities much unless they are available on remote controls.

Tips on using VCRs

1. Make sure that you buy good quality tapes by sticking to well-known makes. If the oxides on the tape are not properly bonded to the backing they can flake off and clog moving parts in the machine.
2. Do not hold the tape on still frame for more than a few minutes. You can clog the heads and damage the tape if you do.
3. Keep cassettes in cases to avoid getting them dusty and dirty.
4. Label your cassettes as soon as you have recorded on to them. It is very easy to lose something you have recorded, especially if you have several tapes.
5. If you have a recording you specially want to keep you can remove the record lockout tab on the tape to make sure you do not accidentally record over it. You can replace the tab later, if you decide to record over it.

†For more about video cameras see pages 6 and 30   ★To find out how infra-red remote controls work see page 17

Using a video camera

To take good pictures with a video camera you need to be aware of the same factors as you would think about if you were using a still camera – focusing, adjusting the amount of light entering your camera and careful positioning of your subject within the edges of your picture. But it also helps to be aware of a few things that apply particularly to taking moving pictures. The great advantage with video is that you can experiment as much as you like without wasting any tape, because you can record on it over and over again.

It is important to keep the camera steady while you are shooting – sequences that jump and jerk about are very difficult to watch. It is often a good idea to rest the camera on a firm surface, or, better still, use a tripod, so that you can turn the camera and tip it up and down while shooting. Some cameras are designed to be hand-held, some to rest on the shoulder. When holding and moving with the camera try to move your whole body as smoothly as possible.

Camera shots

Any programme, whether it is made by professionals or amateurs, is composed of a series of separate shots. A shot is one individual scene. Each time you stop the camera running it is the end of a shot. A good cameraman varies his shots to provide visual interest, taking his subject from several different angles, and distances. You get the best results from planning your shots in advance and thinking how one shot will lead into another. Try to make each shot at least 10 seconds long, if they are any shorter the result will be rather jumpy and fragmented. Here are some of the most basic shots to try out and combine with each other.

A long shot gives the general setting without much detail. It is useful for introducing viewers to a subject and for endings.

In a mid shot the main subject and the background have equal importance.

Close-ups have the most impact on the viewer. All the attention is on one specific thing and the background becomes unimportant. Leave enough room for a border area around the subject.

High angle   **Straight on**   **Low angle**

Another way of varying your shots is to change the height from which you shoot.

The tendency is to shoot from one height (your own or your tripod's) all the time.

Panning is turning the camera from side to side during the shot. Move the camera slowly. A 360 degree pan should take at least one minute. Much faster would confuse the viewer. ▼

◄ With a zoom lens you can move between long shots and close-ups without moving the camera during the shot. Move the zoom slowly and smoothly. Too much zooming can be disturbing to the viewer.

Tilting is tipping the ► camera up or down. It is a good idea to hold the camera still for about three seconds when starting to pan or tilt and when completing the shot.

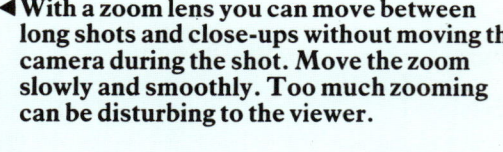

TV in the future

Television is likely to continue on its present course of rapid change into the foreseeable future. All sorts of astonishing innovations are already technologically possible. How soon they will come into general use, or whether they do at all, depends on whether anybody wants to buy them and what they are prepared to pay. In the immediate future, cable and satellite broadcasting are likely to bring about a tremendous increase in the number of TV channels. Stereo sound, more compact equipment and changes in the size and nature of the image on the screen are all likely to follow.

The camera tube in TV and video cameras will eventually be replaced by a light-sensitive silicon chip. This would allow cameras to become very much smaller. Eventually all electronic cameras will probably have a tiny built-in video recording system, just as cine cameras have film inside.

The picture tube in TV sets may also become obsolete. This would mean that sets could be much thinner and could be made both larger and smaller than the present range of sets. People are experimenting with various different systems of creating these "flat screen" televisions.

HDTV

The problem with increasing the size of the screen is that as the picture gets bigger, the detail or "definition" decreases. To solve this problem various systems of producing high-definition television (HDTV) are being developed. They all depend upon increasing the number of lines per picture to over a thousand. Very good results can already be achieved, even when the picture is the size of a large cinema screen. However, an HDTV system requires its own special cameras, TV sets and recorders. It would also require new methods of transmission, probably by satellite because it takes up so much room on the air waves.

3D TV

Three-dimensional television (3D TV) makes the images on the screen look as though they are coming out of the TV towards the viewer. There have already been some quite successful experiments in 3D TV. The viewers have to wear special spectacles, which have a red filter for one eye and a green filter for the other. The picture consists of two images – one superimposed on top of the other. One image is red and one image is green. Through the coloured spectacles each eye can only see one image. This fools the viewer into seeing a single three-dimensional scene in black and white.

TV holography

Another way of recreating 3D images is through holography – a technique which uses laser beams and photographic plates. To make TV holography possible scientists will have to find a practical way of capturing and transmitting moving holograms. Research in this area is very complex and expensive and is still in its early stages.

TV communications

Future technology could turn television into one of the main ways for people to communicate with each other. Already video cameras and cable systems have made it possible for groups of people in different places to hold "meetings" in which they can all take part. Perhaps one day, instead of telephoning someone, you will simply summon their image to the screen and talk into the TV set.

Index

aerial, 5, 14, 28
amplifiers, 14
analogue-digital converter, 24
analogue signal, 24, 25
audio dub, 28
automatic edit, 28

barn doors, 10
Betamax, 29
bidirectional microphones, 9
booms, 9, 11
broadcasting, 4, 5, 14
buses, 13

cable TV, 14, 15
camera tube, 31
cameras, 3, 6, 7, 29, 30
caption rollers, 12
cardioid microphones, 9
carrier waves, 16, 17
cassettes, 29
channels, 17, 29
channel selector, 29
character generators, 12, 25
chromakey, 22, 23
chrominance signals, 8
colour cameras, 8
commentators, 18
computer programs, 27
computers, 2, 24, 25, 26, 27
control desk, 12, 13
control rooms, 5, 10, 11, 12, 18, 22
cuts, 13
cutting room, 21

diaphragm, 9
dichroic mirrors, 8
digital-analogue converter, 25
digital effects, 24, 25
digital paint boxes, 25
digital signals, 24
Direct Broadcast Satellites, 15
director, 10, 11, 12, 19
discs, video 3, 29
dolly, 6
dots on TV screen, 16, 17
double shot, 22, 23
dubbing, 21

edit start button, 21
editing, 20, 21
electronic effects, 22, 23
electronic field production, 19
electronic news gathering (ENG), 18
electronic viewfinder, 6
electron gun, 6, 7, 16
electrons, 7, 16

fibre optic cable, 15
film, 4, 18
film editing, 21
filming on location, 19
films on TV, 17
flat screen TV, 31
floor manager, 11
formats of VCRs, 29
frame advance, 28
frame libraries, 25
freeze-frame, 28
frequency, 14, 17
future TV, 27, 31

ghosting, 15
gun microphone, 18, 19

HDTV, 31
helical system, 20
holography, 31
home computers, 2, 26, 27
home video cameras, 6, 30
home video equipment, 28, 29, 30
home video tape editing, 21

infra red remote controls, 17, 29
interactive TV, 27

land lines, 18
lenses, 7, 8
lines, on TV screen, 7, 16, 17, 31
live broadcasts, 4, 12
loader, 28
luminance signal, 8

MCR, 18
microchips, 2, 3, 24, 26, 31
microphones, 5, 9, 10, 11, 12, 19
microwave radio link, 19
mixes, 13
mixing desk, 23
mobile control room, 18
modem, 27
modulators, 14
monitors, 10, 12, 18, 26
moving coil microphone, 9
moving heads, 20

networks, 15
news gathering, 18
news programmes, 12
NTSC, 8

omnidirectional microphones, 9
optical viewfinder, 6
oscillators, 14
outside broadcasts, 18, 19

"painting by numbers", 23
PAL, 8
panning, 30
pay TV systems, 15
persistance of vision, 17
phosphor, 16
picture tube, 16, 31
portable VCR's, 29
prerecording, 4
preview monitor, 12
production control area, 18
production control room, 10, 12, 13
radio waves, 4, 5, 14, 15, 17, 18
recording, 20
recording heads, 20, 28
relay station, 15
remote controls, 17, 29
roller caption, 25

satellite TV, 14, 15, 31
screen, 16
SECAM, 8

shadow mask tube, 16
shots, 21, 30
sound, 9
sound control room, 10
sound effects, 10
sound engineers, 9, 18
stage manager, 10
stereo sound, 31
studios, 10, 11, 18

target plates, 6, 7, 8, 24
telecine machine, 4, 5, 18
teleprompt, 12
teletext, 27
three dimensional TV, 31
transmission monitor, 12
transmitters, 5, 15, 19
transmitting, 5, 14
tube, camera, 6, 7, 8
tube, TV set, 16
tuners, 17, 28
TV games, 26
TV sets, 16
TV stations, 11

UHF, 14

VCRs, 20, 21, 28, 29
VDU, 26
VHF, 14
VHS, 29
video camera, 29
video discs, 3, 29
video games, 2, 26
video tape, 3, 20, 29
video tape editing, 21
Video 2000, 29
videotext, 27
view data, 27
vision control room, 11
vision engineer, 18
vision mixer, 11, 12, 13
VTRs, 20

wavelength, 14
wipes, 13

zooms lens, 6, 30

First published in 1982 by
Usborne Publishing Ltd, 20 Garrick Street,
London WC2 9BJ, England.
© 1982 Usborne Publishing

The name Usborne and the device are
Trade Marks of Usborne Publishing Ltd.

Printed and Bound in Great Britain
by Purnell and Sons (Book Production) Ltd.,
Paulton, Bristol